# AN APPEAL

# IN ARGENTINA

## *The Apparitions of San Nicolás*

*By* Fr. René Laurentin

*"Undoubtedly, this event of grace will continue to grow; it has proved its authenticity by its spiritual fruits."* (Msgr. Castagna, Bishop of San Nicolás, homily of July 25, 1990)

*Translated from French by*
Juan Gonzalez Jr., Ph.D.
Texas Southern University
Houston, TX 77004

*Edited and Published by*
FAITH PUBLISHING COMPANY
P.O. Box 237
Milford, Ohio 45150

The publisher recognizes and accepts that the final authority regarding the apparitions at San Nicolás rests with the Holy See of Rome, to whose judgment we willingly submit.

The Publisher

Published by Faith Publishing Company
For additional copies, write to:
Faith Publishing Company
Box 237
Milford, Ohio 45150

This book originally published as "UN APPEL DE MARIE EN ARGENTINE," September, 1990, by O.E.I.L., Paris, France.



Library of Congress Catalog Card No.: 90-085751

ISBN: 0-9625975-5-4

# Table of Contents

# Dedication

This book of the apparitions at San Nicolás is offered to Our Lady. May she herself inspire the readers.

The author also expresses his acknowledgement to His Excellency Monsignor Castagna and his episcopal curia who received, documented, and clarified it at the bishopric of San Nicolás.

This study was undertaken through the impetus of Marie Helen Gall and owes much to her examining and compiling of the messages, which she inwardly lives and understands.

The author is also deeply indebted to Father Pérez, rector of the new sanctuary of Our Lady of San Nicolás. It was he who precisely established the first messages and furnished me with the key to their interpretation.

Fr. Pérez would also like to express his gratitude for the attentive translations and additions for this volume, for which he put his inexhaustible zeal to the test.

The apparitions are not dogma; they are not indispensable. They are offered for love. It is up to each to freely discern whether this appeal from Our Lady calls you and becomes for you—as for many—a fountain of life.

With great hesitation and humility, I dare to present a first study of this initiative from Heaven. Messages, graces, prayer and conversions, cures and signs, in great numbers are beyond me. Many times I made improvements to this outline. Theologians of the future will have very much to discover in this gift from Heaven. May this first work communicate what is essential, on its divine level of light and coherence. It has few complications, since it deals with an extremely popular phenomenon among the people of God.

# Publisher's Note

The messages of San Nicolás number over 1,800. There are several different volumes available. Most of these have been published in Argentina in Spanish.

To contact the publisher of the messages in Argentina, write:

"MOVIMIENTO MARIANO" (Marian Movement)
55 Casilla de Correo
2900 San Nicolás (Buenos Aires)
ARGENTINA

In the United States, the messages, in English, are listed in a separate book: "THE MESSAGES OF SAN NICOLÁS." It is being published by Faith Publishing Company. To obtain a copy, write:

FAITH PUBLISHING COMPANY
P.O. BOX 237
MILFORD, OHIO 45150

In this book, AN APPEAL FROM MARY IN ARGENTINA, the messages are shown with a number reference.

Those messages that are shown as "0" followed by a number are from the index of messages compiled by the visionary and recorded in San Nicolás. The number following the "0" is the message number.

Those messages shown as "P" followed by a number are from the index of messages compiled by Fr. Pérez, spiritual director of the visionary, and numbered accordingly.

# Foreword

## *A Call from Mary in the Southern Hemisphere*

In the autumn of 1983, the apparitions of the Blessed Virgin discreetly began in San Nicolás, Argentina. It is located 232 kilometers north of Buenos Aires. It is an historical city, where, on May 31, 1852, the founding agreement of the Argentine Constituent Assembly was signed. It is a city which has been dedicated to the Blessed Virgin Mary for a century. Thousands of prayer groups were founded throughout the country upon listening to this message, and the influence of the apparitions has spread on an international scale.

The visionary remains secluded. Her parish priest watches over her and provides spiritual advice. The bishop guides and channels the fervor of the place and the pilgrimages, in an exemplary pastoral style: no juridical statements, but an effective participation which is modest, critical and fruitful. Bishop Castagna often presides over the monthly procession, and on the anniversary, as many as 100,000 people come, every September 25. He preaches and celebrates Mass. He is building the sanctuary over the site of the apparition, on the bank of the Paraná.

On March 19, 1989, he moved the statue of "Our Lady of the Rosary" there. It had been kept at first in the cathedral. He authorized the start of a women's religious community (normally required to be a diocesan congregation), in the service of this new place of pilgrimage.

The event developed with exceptional harmony at all levels: the people of God, the Bishop, *The Argentine Episcopal Conference.* For once, the apparitions are making their way without becoming a bone of contention. What happened then at San Nicolás?

# San Nicolás, City of Our Lady

## *Soon To Be 400 Years Old*

San Nicolás first appeared as a hamlet and a small parish of the diocese of Rosario. In 1608, Hernando Arias de Saavedra built it into a village. The chapter of Buenos Aires approved this initiative on September 1, 1608.

In the census of 1744, the area had already numbered 948 inhabitants, scattered in five groups along the Paraná River.

On April 14, 1748, Rafael de Aguiar organized the city. For this purpose he donated parcels of property of his spouse Juana Paulina de Ugarte. One of them became the public square, today named "Mire." He built a chapel there dedicated to St. Nicholas of Bari, which was the beginning of the present day Cathedral.

In 1810, San Nicolás sent 357 volunteers for the expeditionary corps in Paraguay.

On March 2, 1811, the first Argentine naval battle took place in the waters of San Nicolás. At the end of this period, troubled by the revolutionary ideas and the struggles which resulted from them, San Nicolás was declared a city on November 3, 1819, by the Constituent General Congress which had convened in Buenos Aires.

On December 6, 1821, a popular vote declared St. Nicholas of Bari, patron saint of the city, according to the desire which had already been expressed by Aguiar in 1748. The commercial port developed in 1833. It was declared a major transit port in 1852. In this same year, the *Accord of San Nicolás* was signed in the city on May 31st. All the governors of the provinces were there in order to establish the constituent assembly which drafted the Constitution, and established the political organization of Argentina.

Two years later, on March 12, 1854, a municipality was established through the reorganization of the local administration. Some names were given to the streets.

In 1857, the first periodical, *La Revista Comercial* appeared; in 1872, the first newspaper, *El Progreso.* On February 3, 1875, the tribunals were set up. In 1876, the *School Council* and the *College of the Salesians* were founded.

In 1888, the development of an extraordinary industrial and commercial banking movement began. Cultural institutions multipled—museums, historical archives, municipal theaters, etc.

The city depended on the diocese of Rosario. On March 3, 1947, San Nicolás became the episcopal seat, suffragan of Rosario, which became the archdiocese.

Today the population has exceeded 140,000 people, and the city known historically as "City of the Accord" (from 1852) and "City of Steel" has become, since September 25, 1983, the "City of Mary," through the apparitions which began on that day. It awakened the faith of all of Argentina and beyond.

## *Who is St. Nicholas?*

St. Nicholas de Myra de Bari was born in Patara, Lycia, about the year 270, and was elected, as a very young man, as bishop of Myra. He suffered Roman persecution and also participated at the *Council of Nicea* in 325. He died about the year 340, and we know very little about him.

Some sailors from Bari hid his body in 1087, and took it to Bari which thus became a great center of pilgrimage. He is venerated as a distinguished miracle worker.

His patronage, popularized by the legend of three small, poor children reduced to starvation, and saved by Nicholas, spread throughout the western world, and then in the New World. We celebrate his feast on December 6th.

In American and trans-Alpine folklore, St. Nicholas became Santa Claus, the old man with a white beard who distributes presents to children at Christmas time.

*CHAPTER 1*

# It Began On September 25, 1983

It all began on September 25, 1983, a date which has since become a holiday, and a day of crowds.

Its beginnings were ignored by everyone. Gladys Herminia Quiroga de Motta was in her room. She was reciting the Rosary. The Blessed Virgin appeared to her. She made a gesture as if to give Gladys her rosary. The apparition was brief: a sort of annunciation.

Gladys, who had become a visionary on that day, was born on July 1, 1937. She is a woman of the lower class, simple, ordinary. She is not comfortable being the center of attention. She maintains discretion and silence in the small oratory which adjoins her house. She is capable of passing unnoticed.

But in spite of the concern to respect her place of seclusion, it is difficult to remain silent about her name and her remarkable existence, for she is the messenger of Our Lady. She has a mission. She is its channel, and its sign. She possesses credibility, as with Catherine Labouré and Bernadette. One more trial for her is the stigmata, which she gladly accepts.

Gladys lives on the outskirts of San Nicolás, in a working class area of low roofed houses. Hers is located on one of the small streets that run at right angles and into a wasteland, the *Campito,* on the bank of the Paraná. This river, already some kilometers wide here, ends in the largest estuary in the world, some 250 kilometers farther down.

Many branches and hundreds of small islands join in this watery network. Hence we have the name of the city: San Nicolás *de los Arroyos,* "of the streams." The proximity of the river has left an area of wasteland on the border of the large industrial city (more than 140,000 inhabitants).

Gladys has two daughters, born in 1961 and 1965. She is now a young grandmother. Her husband, a metal worker until the end of 1989, drove huge cranes in the iron and steel complex of SOMISA, which assisted in the expansion of San Nicolás and attracted other industries to it. He has recently taken an early retirement.

## Antecedents

Prior to September 25, 1983, Gladys had never had an apparition, nor experienced any extraordinary phenomena, either religious, or through a medium.

There was one antecedent—a little more than a month before the apparition. She had seen her rosary, which was hanging in her room, light up. Some neighbors saw it. Thus she began to recite the rosary with them, then by herself. Such was the stage at the time of the first apparition.

Gladys was an average Christian, a normal woman—solid, realistic and optimistic. As a serious but open young woman, she would go dancing once a year, which was not very often in this country where dancing is part of the culture. It was there that she met her husband. Since then, she would go dancing more frequently with him. She still liked to dance until that September 25, 1983, which transferred her tastes to other more spiritual matters.

The first apparition surprised her, but it did not trouble her. She was not afraid. She recognized the Blessed Virgin with the Child, under classic and familiar features. . . transfigured by a living light. What was more natural than for this mother to appear?

Still, Gladys was laconic. She does not speak or write much about the event which transformed her life. She does not write well. She had only four years of elementary school, from age seven to eleven. She wore glasses and reading was difficult for her. Her health was not very good. Like many children, she preferred to leave school and stopped writing ever since. She communicated to me, that never in her life has she ever sent a letter to anyone.

## *First Apparition*

Then why did she feel the need to write on that day? It was to record the sudden event which changed and filled her life: a supernatural meeting. . .and yet so natural, so clear, the blossoming of a beautiful mother. She wrote only these words:

> September 25, 1983:
> (Vi a la Virgen por primera vez):
> "I saw the Blessed Virgin for the first time."

It was a Sunday, a day given to full electoral campaigning for those elections which reestablished democracy in Argentina. It slowly passed for her, in her small home, next to the future sanctuary (Cortada Figari 122).

Gladys immediately recognized the Blessed Virgin. She resembled the classical statues: blue dress, Child in her arms, rosary in hand. Gladys did not speak to anyone about it. She did not have the slightest idea that a priest would call that day—"The beginning of the triumph of Mary." She did not experience any fear, and she had no idea of the duration of the apparition.

Nothing happened on the day after. . .nor did she expect anything. Nothing two days later. . .and she did not expect anything.

## *Other Apparitions*

On September 28, her heart stirred and throbbed. Just as the first time, she was in her room. And here, the Blessed Virgin appeared again, dressed in blue, with the Child Jesus.

She held out her rosary to her. Gladys only wrote:

> (La ví nuevamente):
> "I saw her again." (#0-2).

Then again, on October 5th, in her room, while she was reciting the rosary.

Why these repeated, unusual, unbelievable, and yet supernatural apparitions, Gladys asked herself. "I will ask her the next time." But, the Blessed Virgin has not always spoken.

Gladys continued her life as a housewife, in her little home with green fencing, with a little garden. She kept everything there in perfect order. Nothing happened on October 6th.

## *First Prophetic Message*

And thus it happened that on the following morning, October 7, Feast of the Holy Rosary, the interior warning which she felt, now manifested itself. She instinctively closed her eyes, as usual, saw a light, and immediately, in this light, the same apparition, living and real, with a large rosary in her hands. She observed:

> "I saw her and I asked her what she wanted of me. Then her image faded away and a chapel appeared. I understood that she wanted to be among us (compredí que quería estar entre nosotros)." (#0-3).

The Blessed Virgin answered without words, while showing the prophetic image of the chapel which she desired. This will be her place of residence among us, as God formerly had His tent among the tents of the Hebrews. She does not always speak. Gladys reflected on this first symbolic message.

October 12th, 1983 was the anniversary of the discovery of America (1492), and the first day of the novena of the years (1983-1992) for the preparation of the 500th anniversary. That day, Gladys spoke to her confessor. He is Father Pérez, parish priest of the Cathedral. He listened. He accepted the unusual fact with discretion and perplexity. He hardly knew Gladys. Everything remained in secret, as was appropriate. (#0-4).

## *First Words of the Blessed Virgin*

On Monday, October 13th (anniversary of the last apparition of Fatima), there was a new apparition, the sixth. The Blessed Virgin spoke for the first time:

> *You have been faithful* (Has Cumplido). *Do not be afraid. Come to see me. You will walk* [with your hand] *in my hand, and you will travel over a long road.* (#0-5).

The Blessed Virgin added, for the first time, a biblical reference: *Ezekiel* 2:4-10. Gladys was to find a bible and learn to identify the reference. The text is harsh. In it Our Lord vehemently complains about His rebellious people:

> *Hard-headed children with an obstinate heart.*

It is an invitation to an examination of conscience. Do we deserve the same reproaches? It is also an encouragement, for Gladys obtained without requesting it, a message which the people of Israel regretted for so long a time in frustration. The Blessed Virgin led Gladys to the Holy Scriptures, the Word of God which clarifies all words.

On October 17th, Gladys went to Rosario, the great city of the archbishop. In the eithteenth century, the parish of Rosario (where there was no bishop yet), had begun the care of San Nicolás, at the time a simple, struggling village, under the sign of the rosary.

The city of Rosario, as its name indicates, is dedicated to "Our Lady of the Rosary." Gladys recognized its effigy. A statue in the Cathedral was relatively comparable to the apparition. She also had a rosary in her hands, but the statue was smaller and it was only an image of the shining reality which Gladys had been given to see.

While there, she writes:

> "I closed my eyes and she appeared, very near, great! While I was praying, she spoke to me: *Listen to my words, and make them be heard. I will always be your guide.* A very white, very strong light illuminated everything, and I felt it like a blessing." (#0-6).

## *More Frequent Messages*

Since that time, Gladys received messages more frequently. The first was on October 19th:

> *Those who rebel are unjust, and the humble ones are the servants of the Lord. You seek help. If I give it to you, you will not fear. Nothing will happen to you. The Lord does not leave anything which is haphazard.* (#0-7).

On October 25th, a month to the day after the first apparition, she returned to Rosario. The apparition took place there. Our Lady extended a white rosary to her as she said:

> *Receive this rosary from my hands and keep it forever and ever. You are obedient; I am happy because of it. Rejoice, for God is with you.* (#0-8).

It is like an echo of the Annunciation: *Rejoice. . .the Lord is with you.* (*Lk.* 1:28-30).

The messages continued on subsequent days:

> On the 28th: *May the Lord illuminate the spirit of mankind. Happy are those who are at peace with Him. Always be humble and submissive as you have known how to be to this day. You are my faithful servant and that pleases the Lord.* (#0-9).

On the 30th: *You are my children, needy but loved. It is time to pray, to ask for repentance, and it will be given!*

*Blessed are those who are with the Lord [. . .]. May my seed not be in vain, or my earth without fruit. Glory to the Eternal Father.* (#0-10).

Gladys adds:

> "I saw a green flag with red curtains and yellow fringes, an altar cover of a natural color, bordered with ochre or light purple (ibid)."

The enigmatic image means hope. Does it relate to the chapel which was shown in the fourth apparition? We do not know.

On October 31st, a new message:

> *The gifts of the Lord are inexhaustible. His Wisdom is without end* (no tiene fin). *Call on it and it will not deceive you.*
>
> *I am not inaccessible as many think. Let them extend their hands and they will reach me.*

This message is important, for it is indeed painful that God should seem so far away, since He is so near and so intimate. The lack of faith keeps Him at a distance. It is we who keep Him at a distance.

For the second time, the Blessed Virgin gives support to this with a biblical reference: *Zachariah* 2:8-17, a message overflowing with hope:

> *Jerusalem will be an open city, inhabited by a multitude of people [. . .]. And I will be to it—oracle of Yahweh—a wall of fire all around and I will be its glory.* (#2-9).

The Blessed Virgin seems to designate herself under the sign of Jerusalem, friendly and well protected.

In November, the messages continued, often with reference to Holy Scripture: a new and exceptional fact in the history of the apparitions. Mary leads to the Word of God, and it is a new way for her of continuing her invitation to the servants of Cana: *Do whatever He tells you.* (*Jn.* 2:5).

On November 1st, Gladys experienced a motion from the Holy Spirit. She saw a white light and she heard these words:

> *I am with you.* (#0-12 and Pérez #4).

She refers to *Matthew* 3:16:

> *Immediately after His baptism, Jesus came out of the water and behold the heavens were opened. He saw the Spirit of God descend like a dove and rest upon him. And behold a voice which came from Heaven said: This is My beloved Son, in Whom I am well pleased* (ibid).

On November 3rd, 1983, this gospel text was clearly explained with a passage from St. Paul (*1 Cor.* 1:17):

> *Christ did not send me to baptize but to announce the Gospel, and that without the wisdom of language, so that the Cross of Christ may not be reduced to anything. For the language of the Cross is folly for those who are lost, but for those who are saved, for us, it is the power of God.* (#0-13).

On November 8th, the Blessed Virgin recalls her familiar role:

> *When you are in need of something, have recourse to me and I will answer you. I am happy with you. You are worthy of my trust. Glory to the Lord!* (#0-14).

She also says with reference to the sanctuary, the construction of which she will soon request:

*I will break the rocks, I will excavate the caves* (the crypts of the future Church). *Be persevering then!* (ibid).

On November 12th, she explicitly states the positive aspect of this irruption.

> *You are thirsty for my presence. They will eat from my hands. Be patient; everything will come at its time. Your spirit is nourished by the Holy Spirit. Yours will be the chapel, and it will belong to you* (spiritually. . .). "And I experienced a great aroma of roses," observed Gladys here. (#0-16).

This is what the message of June 27, 1987, (#1210) will explain:

> *Those who experience the perfume of my roses walk with me.*

The Blessed Virgin adds:

> *You are not very weak. You have the faith. Your cross is heavy, but you know how to carry it.* ("Here I experienced a strong smell of incense." (#0-16).)

Roses announce the rosary, and incense, sacrifice.

## Some Daily Messages

Beginning in mid November, the apparitions and messages are no longer sporadic, but daily. Some remain private, but more than 1800 have been published (exactly 1804 according to the official count). The first messages have been omitted.

## First Written Messages

On November 15th, Christ spoke for the first time, in a more brief and succinct style.

> *I am the sower. Gather the harvest; it will be great.* (Pérez #6).

On November 16th, the Blessed Virgin told Gladys:

> *I am patroness of this region. Assert my rights.* (Pérez #6).

This message recalls that the parish of San Nicolás, care of Rosario, was entrusted to "Our Lady of the Rosary" from the beginning. The people placed their filial trust in her. Her statue had been in a prominent place in the cathedral, which had been opened in 1884. It was a gift from Señora Carmen Acevedo de Insurradle. It had been brought from Rome after it had been blessed by Pope Leo XIII. For the inauguration, this Virgin with the Child has a blue and pink mantle and a white mantilla on her head. The wooden statue is of a slightly taller size than that of an ordinary woman. It was at that time that they established the "Brotherhood of the Rosary" which was preparing for the feast, with a novena.

But an accident had broken the hand which held the Rosary, and the statue had been relegated to the church tower while waiting to be repaired, which did not occur. The Blessed Virgin insisted:

> *I want to be near you* (near the river). *Water is a blessing.*

Gladys asked, "Do you want a chapel or a sanctuary?" The Blessed Virgin answered:

> *Holy Scriptures say it.*

And she referred her to *Exodus* 25:8: "They will make me a sanctuary, and I will dwell in the midst of them."

> *Carry out my word.*

On the morning after, November 17th, Jesus spoke for the second time in the same succinct manner.

> *Glorious days await you. You will rejoice in me, my beloved children.* (Pérez #8).

The same day Our Lady invited Gladys to speak to the bishop: *Announce my request.* (Pérez #7).

On the 19th, she confirms her mission to her:

> *You are a bridge of unity. Preach my word. Many will be the people who are blind who do not want to see. Many will be the deaf who do not want to hear. But do not be weak! For yours is the kingdom of Heaven.*

## *A Ray of Light*

On the night of November 24th, Gladys went with a group of people to the place chosen by Mary to build her shrine, and while she was showing them the site where she saw the apparition, a powerful ray of light fell on this spot and seemed to disappear into the ground. A nine-year-old girl (whom her family has kept incognito) also saw the ray.

On the morning after, the 25th, the Blessed Virgin told Gladys:

> *The Holy Spirit is your guide. You must obey. This is the place of my residence. Everything rests in your hands.* (Pérez #17).

Then she confided to her:

> *I suffered very much as Mother. But the Almighty has rewarded me for eternity. I am close to my adorable Son, for the glory of mankind, with the grace of the Lord. Amen.*

She invited Gladys to read the *Acts of the Apostles* 6:7-8 and 8:8:

> *Thus the word of God spread more each day. The number of disciples increased considerably in Jerusalem, and many priests embraced the faith. They were there, full of grace and power and did great prodigies and signs among the people.*

*And the joy of this city was great!* (ibid).

Vocation and a bright outlook for San Nicolás!

Two days later on the 26th, the Blessed Virgin told Gladys:

> *Your abandonment* (entrega) *is complete. Be blessed. Your mission is great. You do not know the dimension of it.* (Pérez #18).

Gladys asked her:

> "Would you like for us to call you 'Our Lady of the Rosary of San Nicolás?'"
> *So it is that you must say. My wish is to be among you, to fill you with blessings, with peace, joy and to bring you closer to God Our Lord.*

The biblical reference of this day (*Col.* 3:15) begins thus:

> *May the peace of Christ reign in your hearts; this peace to which you have been called because we form one single body. Live in thanksgiving!*

On November 27th, a pilgrim image of Christ arrived in San Nicolás, where the novena to the patron saint began. The Blessed Virgin said:

> *Today is a day of joy for all of you. Go and honor Our Lord. I will be in the midst of you.*
> *Gather and grow in the faith. That is what Our Lord asks. You are a great flock. He is its great shepherd. Glory to the Lord!*
> *Blessed be the people of San Nicolás for the great faith which they have placed in God and in its patron saint. Nothing should worry you. Everything is in my hands.* (Pérez #19).

She immediately invited her to read the *Epistle of St. James,* beginning with chapter 1, vs. 5:

*If any of you are lacking in wisdom, let him ask God for it, and he will receive it, for He gives it to all generously without demanding anything in return.*

## *From Rejection to Honor*

It was on this same day that Father Pérez learned that the statue of "Our Lady of the Rosary," which had been located at the cathedral for a long time, was in the belfry. It coincided with Gladys' description. So he had the visionary come, and led her to the belfry to see it. She was astonished. She immediately recognized the apparition, and immediately the Blessed Virgin appeared to her, in front of the statue, and said to her:

*They had kept me in oblivion, but I reappeared. Put me up again since you see me just as I am.* (11/27/83, Pérez #20).

At that moment, Gladys saw, behind the statue, the stained glass window of the Holy Trinity with the angels, and the Blessed Virgin said:

*I want to settle on the bank of the Paraná. Be strong. There, you have seen my light. May your strength not weaken. Glory be to the Father Most High!*

So, she is going to leave the cathedral, her place of origin, for a larger audience, for the good of the diocese, and for all of Argentina.

Father Pérez had the statue repaired, and placed in her hands and in those of her Son, a new rosary. Consequently, a procession began in the cathedral, in front of the patroness of the city. Hosts of orphans found a mother again, and came to visit her with joy.

*CHAPTER 2*

# Ecstasies?

Since November 27, 1983, Gladys has seen almost every day (at home and not at Campito, as we have said) and receives frequent messages. She does not know at what time it will happen:

> "I experience something like a tingling sensation in my arms. Then I know that she is coming. I close my eyes and she appears."

She also receives frequent messages. They come to her inwardly. And if she is with others, she gives no indication of the event. Her prayer group guesses it, when she closes her eyes.

It seems that with her, there is no ecstacy strictly speaking, in the sense of a separation from the external world. This is in contrast to Kibeho and Medjugorje, where the visionaries cease to see and to hear what surrounds them after the beginning of the apparition. A brilliant perception of another world obscures the world here below. Gladys' perception is tangible, real, surrealistic. But she frees herself from the external world, simply by closing her eyes.

Are we to say then, that it is a matter of an internal and subjective vision? No. For Gladys the Blessed Virgin is real, living. She has touched her. She has felt the firmness and warmth of her body, not through ordinary perception, but according to a more direct, more existential way, no less real, but surrealistic. It commands a linking of coherent reactions—a listening, and response in a very real intimacy. At times, those around her perceive a sweet smell of roses and a feeling of warmth.

*CHAPTER 3*

# Our Lady Leads To The Bible

The messages are often accompanied by an invitation to read Holy Scripture. The Blessed Virgin often gave a reference; at first this troubled Gladys.

A finicky exegete, who was sent on the technical demands of his discipline, conducted a statistical and critical examination of these references (89 to the Old Testament, and 148 to the New Testament). The most frequent are:

> *For the Old Testament:* Isaiah (16 times); Psalms (15); Deuteronomy (the law of love: 10); then Job, Proverbs, Wisdom, Ecclesiastes (6 times).
>
> *For the New Testament:* the Epistle to the Hebrews (16 times); Romans (14); the Gospel of St. John (11 times), the Acts of the Apostles and Matthew (9 times); the First Epistle of Peter (8 times); the Apocalypse and the Epistle of James (7 times); the First Epistle to the Corinthians and the Gospel of St. Mark (5 times), and that of Luke (3 times).

The exegete notes that these references are arbitrary. It is in fact, a spiritual exegesis, the invitation to a "living reading" of Holy Scripture, of which the Old and then the New Testaments give testimony. It is characterized by a concern to apply the texts to contemporary life, for the Bible illuminates life and life illuminates the Bible.

It is a matter then of recovering the possession of the Word of God in the present moment, and the present moment from this Word. For there is a reciprocal light between the Word of God and the life of man which it guides. From this symbol (Greek, *sum-bolos,* as Holy Scriptures say), God creates a spark of light. That is what we call *midrash.* The Virgin Mary practiced it according to St. Luke. She meditated on the words and the events of the childhood of Christ, and "pondered them in her heart," say Holy Scriptures (*Lk.* 2:19 and 51).

The first text (*Lk.* 2:19) expresses this illuminating "pondering" by the word *symballousa* (from the same root as symbol). Mary gives a beautiful example of it in the *Magnificat,* literally weaved with former biblical formulas, which now carry a new meaning in light of the Annunciation.

The Angel Gabriel addressed Mary on recalling the biblical prophecies which he actualized. His first words:

> *Rejoice, full of grace, the Lord is with you. . . Do not be afraid, Mary. . .*

are a summation of the prediction of Zephaniah (*Soph.* 3:14-17):

> *Rejoice, you daughter of Zion. Yahweh, King of Israel, is in your bosom.*
> *Do not be afraid, Zion, [. . .]*
> *Yahweh your God is in your womb, valiant Savior.*

This prophesy of the new dwelling place of God for His people, finds an extraordinary fulfillment in Mary and, therefore, already expressed through the prophecy: the Incarnation:

> *Behold you will conceive and bear in your womb [. . .] the Son of the Most High [. . .], the Son of God.* (*Lk.* 1:31-35).

At the beginning of the *Magnificat,* mixed with biblical verses, Mary takes up the words from *Habakkuk* 3:18:

*My soul exults in God, my Savior.*

She gives new meaning to these words of the prophet in terms of what has just been announced. She has "conceived a Son." She must "give Him the name Jesus" which means Yahweh, the Savior. The Hebrew of the prophet Habakkuk can be translated:

> *My soul exults in God my Savior,* or *in God my Jesus.*

St. Jerome preferred the latter translation for *Habakkuk* 3:18, taken up by Mary in her *Magnificat.*

In brief, the announcement to Mary was interspersed (illuminated) with biblical re-uses: the old texts clarified the new event, and the new event clarified the old texts, fulfilled in an unexpected and complete way.

That is what Mary continues to do in San Nicolás.

Biblical revelation progressed in this manner throughout the Old Testament, through successive fulfillments of Holy Scripture in terms of new events. These re-uses were called *Midrash.*

These understandings were arbitrary, if you want, but still inspired by God and according to the dynamics of hope, which makes the future rise from the Word itself. It is thus that the Blessed Virgin invites Gladys to read the Holy Scripture. She tells Gladys on January 27, 1984:

> *Through these messages and the Holy Scriptures, the Lord will reveal to you what He expects of mankind.* (1/27/84, #32).

It is then, a living, prophetic exegesis turned toward the future, which projects the biblical marvels of God on the present day Church for the fulfillment of the plans of the Lord. This very concrete method exposes itself to the literal criticism of scholars, but it contributes to prove that there is no exegete behind Gladys' references. She refers to the living Bible. The people of God exist therein, according to the usual traditions.

Holy Scripture reveals a new reality, not through magic, but because God continues to fulfill His saving plan according to the same structure (the same typology), through movements of the same Holy Spirit. Thus today, we can again call upon the Holy Scriptures, the eternal plan of God, Who invites us to fulfillment in His new creation, according to the same model.

*CHAPTER 4*

# Where The Sanctuary Begins

On January 4, 1984, three months and some days after the first apparition, for the second time, a ray of light came to illuminate the point which would become the ground of the new sanctuary. A slab commemorates it today.

On May 22nd, Our Lady stated precisely:

> *Your mother claims her dwelling place. No luxury. . .but a spacious house.* (#148).

On September 25, 1984, anniversary of the first apparition, Father Pérez instituted the perpetual rosary in the cathedral. The attendance there was considerable, both day and night. The Blessed Virgin gave a grateful message on that day:

> *This day will be resplendent and glorious for your souls. My dear children, as I have asked you, pray and give thanks to the Lord. Also I feel very close to your hearts and I verify that your faith is increasing. Obedience and love which you have for God will not fall into oblivion, I guarantee you. Ask, for God listens to you. Alleluia.* (#298).

This same day she recommended the construction which she had very dear to her heart:

> *Do not forget the sanctuary, because it is a sanctuary of the Lord. Time will pass away, but it will remain.* (#299).

It is a motiff which returns constantly. We will cover it in Chapter 10—"The Message."

*Construction of the Sanctuary*

1. The principal messages relating to the sanctuary are the following:

May 22, 1984 . . . . . . . . . . . . . . . . . . . . no. 148
November 23, 1984 . . . . . . . . . . . . . . . no. 383
December 5, 1984 . . . . . . . no. 398 (identical)
December 18, 1984 . . . . . . . . . . . . . . . no. 414
February 2, 1985 . . . . . . . . . . . . . . . . . no. 463
September 25, 1986 . . . . . . . . . . . . . . no. 976
October 14, 1987 . . . . . . . . . . . . . . . . no. 1277
October 20, 1987 . . . . . . . . . . . . . . . . no. 1281
April 9, 1988 . . . . . . . . . . . . . . . . . . . . . no. 1391
April 12, 1988 . . . . . . . . . . . . . . . . . . . . no. 1395
April 22, 1988 . . . . . . . . . . . . . . . . . . . . no. 1400
March 19, 1989 . . . . . . . . . . . . . . . . . . . no. 1626
October 7, 1989 . . . . . . . . . . . . . . . . . . no. 1728

*CHAPTER 5*

# The Stigmata

The "spring" of 1984 (that is, October-November, the autumn in the northern hemisphere) marks a new stage in Gladys' life.

## *A Prophetic Diagnosis*

Her mission required union with the Passion of Christ, with His suffering. The priest who directed her, sensed it. On October 23, 1984, he sent this penetrating and perceptive report to the bishop:

> "Gladys does not refuse the physical and moral sufferings in that she understands them to be necessary for God's plan and for Redemption. Gradually, she understands all that, and, in these last months, her silence has become more pronounced. It is basically an interior silence. She learns to be silent in her home and even with her rare guests. Her growing interior dialogue with the Lord makes her more silent, to the detriment of the desire of communicating what she is living.
>
> "Beyond the prophetic dimension which God grants her for the service of the community, I believe that she has been called to live the state of a victim. In this reality, the great sufferings of the Passion and her internal fire could take place [. . .]. The wound of love, and the afflic-

tion of love, of which St. John of the Cross speaks, clarifies all that very much, and makes one think at least of similar possibilities."

This diagnosis was prophetic.

## *They Have Nailed My Hands*

Three weeks later, on Friday, November 16, 1984, Gladys experienced the terrible sufferings of the Passion. The stigmata appeared progressively on her wrists. They will renew themselves every Thursday and Friday, during Advent of that year; then each Lent since then.

The doctors (sent by the bishop), Dr. Eduardo Juan Telechea, cardiologist, and Carlos M. Pellicciotta, have carefully examined the phenomenon.

First of all, they see a red spot (hematoma) appear. It is not located on the palm of the hand (as the majority of those who suffer the stigmata), but on the wrist. According to the anatomical truth of the Passion, a body nailed by the palms would not hold up. In the 1930's, Dr. Barbet confirmed that the tissues would tear. Since then, the archeological discovery of a crucifix in Israel has confirmed that the Roman soldiers nailed the wrists. Dr. Barbet identified this point beginning with the impressions of the Shroud. And his studies have revealed the most terrible of the sufferings of the Passion: "the nail driven into this place crushes and severs the median nerve." It thereby causes the most atrocious pain possible. The lesion of this nerve itself, center of painful sensitivity, produces suffering in the most unbearable degree: a flash of interior fire inflames the hand completely: a burning more terrible than would be that of a furnace.

Dr. Barbet verified that the blow to the median nerve would cause the thumb to bend toward the inside of the hand, and that would explain why the thumb was not visible on the imprint of the hand, observable on the shroud (P. Barbet *La Passion de Notre Seigneur Jesus Christ selon le chirurgien,* Issoudum, Dillen, 1950).

It is the same with Gladys. When "the ulceration of the wrist" appeared (that is, the sore strictly speaking: a wound from 1 to 2 centimeters wide), her thumb began to bend, facing the palm of her hand, according to the reflex observed by Barbet. The deeper the ulceration, the more the thumb would react and would sink in. This was visible in one of the pictures. This detail surprised and overwhelmed the doctors.

I asked Gladys if she previously knew of the Shroud of Turin. She had no recollection of it.

> "Yes," she observed, while hunting for it, "there was a conference on that at the church."
> "Was it before or after your stigmatization?"
> "I do not know."

She had no knowledge of any studies about the shroud, and had not made the comparison which I referred to her. The stigmatization of the two hands did not have the same development. This also goes along with the meaning of anatomical truth.

The two doctors analyzed the blood in order to be sure that there was no intervention of any dye. Their observations excluded all trickery.

The physical pain is great, but the moral suffering is still greater, according to Gladys, who joins other mystics in this belief.

The stigmata of the hands are given to Gladys during Advent and Lent, but blood flows only on Fridays in Lent.

## . . . And My Feet

The doctors also observed the stigmata of the feet. They occur only on Good Friday.

They begin a little after 3 in the afternoon—the hour of the death of Christ—as if to stress that it is a matter of fulfilling what is lacking in His sufferings for His Body, which is the Church (*Col.* 1:24).

The stigmata of the feet do not have the characteristic of wounds. The skin is colored red from the blood which shows on the surface, but without ulceration or flow.

Gladys' left foot comes to place itself on the right foot, as if both feet were nailed with only one nail. The doctor has tried to separate the two feet, which were united. But when he took the left foot in his hands, in order to raise it, the right foot (located below) would follow, as if both belonged to only one limb. He tried to place his hand between the two superimposed legs, at the level of the knees; he was not successful. That seemed all the more unexplainable as there was no muscular contraction, either of the calf or of the thigh, to justify this position. There was no contraction or voluntary resistance. The muscles were perfectly relaxed.

**Counterproof:** When the doctor produced a rotary movement of the left leg, the two feet turned as one piece. They seemed to be glued. If he turned the left foot on the side, the other foot would follow.

Briefly, the doctor whom I questioned, concluded:

1. The constant muscular relaxation, during rest as well as when she raised her left leg, excluded any voluntary or simulated movement.

2. In the same way, the absense of muscular contraction in the calf, which must be contracted when the foot is stretched. The muscles of the calves are completely relaxed, flaccid.

## *Carrying of the Cross and Transfixion*

On Good Friday, Gladys particularly experiences the carrying of the cross. Her shoulder is marked with an extended, very painful spot.

At times, it is the transfixion: a wound opens up on the side, without a flow of blood.

The maximum suffering for her is that of the right hand, as if it were broken, crushed.

*CHAPTER 6*

# Fasting

A little after the first stigmata (November 16, 1984), Gladys was invited to fast for thirty days during Advent. An almost complete fast. She had anticipated it, perhaps of her own accord. The year before, from November 1 to December 1, 1983, she had eaten very little during the five days which preceded, and during that month took only a little grapefruit juice, and once a day some tea or coffee with cream.

For her, it was not a penance; it was a purification. She did not experience hunger at all. That might be relatively normal for one who fasts without reflecting on himself. But Gladys presented a remarkable uniqueness: the attraction for food disappeared.

— "You cooked for your husband during those days. Did it not make you hungry?"
— "No, during the fast, I lose the sense of smell and there is no appetite."
— *The Holy Spirit nourishes you,* the Blessed Virgin told her.

The lenten fast lasts 40 days and, in spite of the very small quantities of food, she lost only three and a half pounds. Her normal weight is 136 pounds and her height is 5′3″ according to the doctors.

It is astonishing, for in fasting on water alone, one loses on an average of a kilo a day during the first week. A little less during the following weeks (500 to 200 grams on an average).

It can be relatively explained. It happens that during an extended fast, the rest of the pancreas causes a decrease of insulin (hypo-insolumenia). That causes the level of sugar to rise (hyperglycemia), and this level, higher than normal, maintains weight while the intestinal and pancreatic system is at rest.

## *A Request from Our Lady*

"It is the Blessed Virgin who invited me to fast," Gladys explicitly told me. But only one of the 1804 messages which have been published, invite her to it without preciseness.

January 11, 1989.

> *My child, yesterday it was at Lourdes; today it is here, but it is always good for the mother to be in search of her children. I expect of them prayer, fasting, conversion.*
>
> *They will find salvation if they do not flee from the Lord; if they accept the Lord.*
>
> *Many souls lack peace. If the soul looks for peace, it will find God.* (#1594).

This message summarizes the one from Lourdes. But it is significant that the Blessed Virgin adds fasting to it as one of the privileged forms of penance.

The fast requested by the Blessed Virgin is not without surprise. Two adolescents from Kibeho, Africa (Segatasha and Anathalie), made an extended fast—without water! The doctors were ill at ease. That should have been fatal before long. They wanted to stop the fast, but the visionaries answered:

— "Our Lady asked us for it. It is she whom we should obey."

It turned out well, contrary to every expectation. Furthermore, at the end of the fast, the visionaries took up normal nourishment without a transition. That should have caused some catastrophe. But they were very well, again, contrary to medical norms, well established for the average person.

## *Renourishment*

I asked Gladys:

— "At the end of the fast, do you renourish yourself suddenly or rather gradually?"
— "After the fast, I am not hungry and I eat little. I experience the need for it less and less."

Her husband worries over this woman who hardly eats. And yet, her complexion is normal without emaciation, as without obesity. She has the fresh complexion of those who eat healthy food, like the Hebrew pages of Nabuchodonosor. The stewards wanted to impose on them the food of the royal table, in order to maintain their good appearance. They refused, and their appearance was better than that of the others. (*Deut.* 1:13-15).

*CHAPTER 7*

# Cures

## *Gonzalo Miguel*

In this same autumn, Monsignor Castagna questioned himself regarding these events from which so many graces flowed, according to information from the curé of his cathedral. He wanted a definite sign. It was then that the first remarkable cure in the history of San Nicolás took place: a cure which is still under study. This is how it happened:

On Friday, October 19, 1984, little Gonzalo Miguel Godoy, 7 years old (born January 14, 1977), and who lived in Pergamino (70 kilometers from San Nicolás), showed the first symptoms of an illness which prostrated him. He was exhausted, laconic, a little restless. He did not speak.

On Thursday, October 25, 1984, a tomography showed evidence of a tumor in the brain. A left frontal lesion exerted pressure on all of this area, and resulted in a paralysis of the right side. The mother, Maria del Valle, called Mariqui, placed herself in the hands of Our Lady and asked for strength to bear the inevitable, for the prognosis was somber. At best, it would require an operation which would leave the child handicapped, if it did not result in death.

The mother was then pregnant with her seventh child. She was in her seventh month. A terrible anxiety overwhelmed her. Then, to her surprise, she found herself immediately seized with a great peace.

On Monday, October 29th, the right side of the child was completely paralyzed. He was in bed, unable to move, cold as death. An arteriography of the brain, made this same day, confirmed his grave condition.

His parents asked for Extreme Unction and First Communion for him at the point of death. Monsignor Castagna granted it. On October 30, 1984, at 10:30, Father Ariel David Busso, chancellor, a friend of the family, came from the diocese. He explained to the child that he was going to receive Jesus. He placed him under the protection of "Our Lady of the Rosary of San Nicolás." The child welcomed this gift from God "with great interior strength." He looked at the Host with his large eyes before receiving Holy Communion.

And it was here that he began to show an improvement: 45 minutes later the paralysis appreciably regressed. The child regained his color. He came out of his torpor. On November 1, 1984, a second tomography verified that the tumor had been reduced by 70 percent. The area of hypodensity was reduced by 70 percent. There was no longer a mass effect, that is, the suppression of the left lateral ventricle by the tumor.

On Friday, November 2nd, there was a lumbar puncture for further analysis. Little Gonzalo offered this suffering to Jesus Whom he had received. He endured the puncture without complaint. The sample did not show any abnormality.

On Saturday, November 3rd, they reduced the medication. The child awakened. He began to play. During the following days, improvement continued. He read. On Wednesday, November 8th, they completely stopped cortisone and medication. The child still remained weakened on the right side.

On Friday, November 9th, Gonzalo walked alone:

> "We could leave the hospital and return home," observed his mother. (See appendix #2).

On Monday, November 19, 1984, the third tomography showed that where there had been a tumor, only a scar was left.

On the following June 2nd, the newspaper *La Nacion* (Buenos Aires), gave an account of the cure, but changed the name of the child to that of Martin, out of discretion. On September 25, 1985, the newspaper *El Norte* published a lengthy article.

The medical study continues to be embarrassed by the disappearance of the first file, which had been gathered by the doctors on this remarkable case. Gonzalo is going to school. He plays heartily. He has friends. He is happy to live and to give thanks for his cure.

## *Other Cures*

Ever since then, a large number of cures have been made public at the sanctuary. Many pilgrims have recorded them spontaneously, in the Book of Testimonies *(Libro de Testimonios),* of which 187 pages had been filled by the end of 1989. Some files have been prepared on certain cases, but it would be premature to describe them in detail before they are complete and studied. Let us give only some examples of these cures, for which the beneficiaries simply give thanks, as the man born blind did, in the Gospel.

Filomena Grande, 52 years of age, from San Miguel de Tucuman: In October 1985, she was seized with hepatic colic. Ultrasound revealed some stones. The doctors recommended an operation, but Mrs. Grande refused and she entrusted herself to Our Lady of San Nicolás.

— "She will indeed know how to remove these stones."

Since the end of 1985, the pains have ceased. The ultrasound, which has been taken since then, is normal. New examination in April, 1986, with perfect results.

Little Juan Ignacio Cordero Olguin, 9 months of age, caught meningitis with cross paralysis: blind, deaf, mute, unconscious, in a comatose state for 9 days, wakes up on the tenth day in a perfect state of health, following prayers addressed to "Our Lady of the Rosary of San Nicolás." Later, medical consultations confirmed the cure. Testimony was signed by Celia C. De Olguin on November 24, 1987.

Anabella Rence Rao (12 years old), a school girl, was seized with paralysis and loss of reflexes in her two lower limbs, December 14, 1988. The neurologist hospitalized her and performed a lumbar puncture. The analysis of the cephalo-rachidian liquid showed a hyperproteinorachy (excess of proteins: 2.89 grams per liter). He diagnosed the Guillain-Barre syndrome. The deterioration stopped on December 17th. On the 24th she could move again, alone and without help. In January 1989, the improvement increased; the retraining was accelerated. On February 7th, Anabella walked normally.

The girl and her mother had put everything in the hands of "Our Lady of the Rosary of San Nicolás" since the diagnosis of December 14, 1988, with the assurance that she "would protect them under her mantle." The sick girl prayed the Angelus continuously and asked God to make her accept what Mary wanted. The novena had begun on December 17th, the day when the progress of the illness suddenly stopped. This recuperation, *ad integrum,* in such a short time, constitutes a clinical exceptional case and contrary to developmental prognosis according to the judgment of regular doctors.

Doctors in San Nicolás have established a medical bureau of specialists to study these continuing cures. It is further described in Appendix #4.

*CHAPTER 8*

# An Exemplary Pastoral

Bishop Castagna is truly a spiritual and good bishop whose main problem is not juridical, but pastoral. Bishop Castagna devotes himself to discernment and the signs are good. He discreetly guides the movement of fervor, which had entirely rested on Fr. Pérez, priest of the cathedral at the time of the first apparitions, and today director of the new sanctuary. He remains vigilant, and tactfully assumes the criticisms and barbs which always come in similar cases.

## *The Pilgrim Bishop*

On March 25, 1986, the feast of the Annunciation, the bishop of San Nicolás participated for the first time in the monthly ceremony which brings together a very fervent crowd. From the first words of his sermon, he takes this pilgrimage upon himself by saying "us" (not the "us" of majesty, but the "us" of solidarity; that of his common prayer with his people):

> "The presence of the Blessed Virgin makes us pilgrims and penitents. It is always she who gives us Jesus our Savior and teaches us to be faithful to the Gospel. The invocations, diversified by the vast tradition in the Church, show the how of her presence which new forms of maternal solicitude manifest unceasingly.

> "Our Lady of the Rosary, in her old and beautiful statue [the statue at the cathedral recognized by Gladys] has conquered the hearts of true multitudes. Through her, God lavishes innumerable graces which, far from ceasing, seem to multiply themselves in a providentially stable manner. The extraordinary crowd of pilgrims concentrates on the sacred statue in this humble place, in our privileged city of San Nicolás."

Such was the first participation, and the first sermon of the bishop of the place. The last words manifested his attentive prudence:

> "As pastor I want to respond to the call of our mother and to recognize her presence, all the while discerning what comes from her, and what exaggerations and deviations can bring about."

It was March 25th. Life in the place of pilgrimage of San Nicolás is attuned to the anniversary of the first apparition, the twenty-fifth of each month. This day is preceded by a novena, maintained through the messages, and the novena ends with a procession followed by Mass, which brings together 100,000 persons and more, especially on September 25th.

## *The Foundation Stone*

On August 25, 1986, five months after his first participation in the monthly procession, the bishop did it again. As the first time, he preached about Our Lady according to the Gospel, without explicit reference to the apparitions. But he created some suspense when he concluded:

> — "And now I am going to tell you something which I have not told anyone until now. It will be a surprise for many. Recently they asked me: *What are you going to do* (Que mas?)

> "And they asked the Blessed Virgin:
>
> — *What do you wish of this poor bishop on whom this heavy heritage has fallen? Is he going to remain hidden, swallowed up in the midst of so many graces?*
>
> "Well, indeed, on the twenty-fifth of next month, I am going to plant in the field, like a seed, the foundation stone. It will be the corner-stone of the house of the Blessed Virgin, which will be our home. There will be no godfather. The godfather will be the people of God: the small and the great."

Neither mounted sentry nor outstanding benefactor: instead the bishop makes the people of God totally responsible for the material and spiritual construction, whose financing is difficult in the terrible economic crisis of Argentina with runaway inflation, and increasing privations which each one must impose on himself. The apparitions come to radiate peace in a difficult situation.

The following month, September 25, 1986, third anniversary of the first apparition, the bishop lays the foundation stone:

> "This stone symbolizes Jesus. It is the corner-stone of the history of each one of us and of all men. Failing that, every construction would be built on sand and the result would ultimately be tragic. That is what we want to keep away from our lives," stated the bishop.

For the first time Bishop Castagna invoked: "Mary of the Rosary of San Nicolás" (#21, p. 20).

And he was precise:

> "The development of the event offers us the certainty that God manifests a special providence in it, through the means of the Blessed Virgin. In my recent pastoral meeting with the people

> of my diocese, especially with the poorest, the profound rootage of this devotion to the Blessed Virgin surprised me. It manifests itself through the filial veneration of this holy image [the statue of Our Lady] and the multiplication of prayer groups among men and young people: they use the prayer of the Holy Rosary [. . .]
>
> "With this cornerstone, we confirm, in virtue of an imprescriptible ministry, the determined expression of the faith of the people in the maternal intercession of the Most Blessed Virgin. We accept the responsibility that this remarkable fact does not deviate, and that the word may not lack for interpretation, or the grace of the sacraments of the Church, which authentically nourishes it." (ibid, #23, p. 20).

In San Nicolás, one breathes easy, thanks to this pastoral awareness of the bishop. Instead of remaining aloof with respect to this vital phenomenon, he assumes responsibility for it, guides it, nourishes it. He watches with an experienced, critical sense, but is concerned above all with stimulating the movement of grace, instead of fighting it as has very often happened for a century. Discouragements and old conflicts have resulted in places where apparitions could have borne fruit, if one would have pruned and directed it, instead of fighting and uprooting it.

Not that all the apparitions which have been repressed have been authentic, but the purely negative attitudes were often fruitless and harmful. San Nicolás is in the process of establishing the contrary.

On December 11, 1987, the bishop reacted in a similar calm manner, to a triple sacrilegious attempt against three images of the Blessed Virgin, of which one was in El Campito. He regarded these sacrilegious acts as satanic actions, in opposition to the influence of Our Lady. He invited people to a peaceful and vigilant protest:

"For we are in the midst of a Marian year, and Mary is our mother. We cannot allow her to be insulted with impunity. We do not claim actions against anyone. But it is simply a matter of awakening consciences." (Declaration of 12/11/87, p. 3).

He decided to lead the prayer of reparation at the time of the procession, the following December 25th, Christmas Day:

"We offer our suffering in view of the abuse committed against Mary, and we will draw from it new energies for evangelization."

## *The Pilgrim Archbishop*

Two months after the laying of the foundation stone, on the anniversary of the first apparition, Bishop Jorge M. Lopez, archbishop of Rosario (of which Bishop Castagna is suffragan), went to San Nicolás in order to confirm the grace which was bearing fruit. He wrote on the following December 11th:

"On November 25th, I went to San Nicolás in order to venerate the Blessed Virgin of the Most Holy Rosary, whose statue is found in the Cathedral.

"I was only a pilgrim like the others, who wanted to renew his trust in and filial love for the mother of Heaven, and pray for her for the needs of the archdiocese [. . .] and of the whole world. It was also the visit of the metropolitan archbishop of which San Nicolás is a suffragan diocese, in order to show my support and my approval of the principles and direction of my dear bishop of San Nicolás, Msgr. Domingo Salvador Castagna, on the subject of the apparitions and the messages of the Most Holy Virgin to Mrs. Gladys de Motta, living in this city. Since I had wished it for a long time [. . .], I wanted to confirm the apostolic prudence of which the bishop of this diocese gave evidence, during this long period.

"The reality of this extraordinary event, on the spiritual level, was imposing of itself without any uncalled for great haste.

"As a result of all this, I was able to gather the comforting impression of a solid, discreet and strong piety, which prevails in the atmosphere as well as during the procession which accompanied the venerated statue of the cathedral to the "Campito of the Blessed Virgin" during the celebration of the Holy Mass [. . .]. During the procession, songs of praise alternated with the recitation of the most Holy Rosary. During the celebration of the Holy Mass, the teaching of the diocesan bishop, the Eucharistic climate, the participation of the faithful, and the fervor of numerous communions, breathed a true presence of the Lord in this crowd which humbly and lovingly surrounded the Most Blessed Virgin of the Rosary.

"The liturgical blessing of the new altar, as well as the building site prepared to erect the large temple in this place whose construction the Blessed Virgin requested [. . .], gave me the certainty that this work of great scope would soon be a reality [. . .]. The devotion, constantly stimulated by the messages of the Blessed Virgin, claims the conversion and holiness of all.

"May she always wish to receive the numerous pilgrims who come to San Nicolás (in *Revista del Santuario,* December 1987, p. 14).

## *Welcome by the Argentine Episcopacy*

Bishop Castagna informed the Episcopal Conference. It showed itself extremely favorable, for many bishops had already confirmed in their dioceses the excellence of these fruits.

*CHAPTER 9*

# The Delay Required By Mary

After some difficulties (for the Blessed Virgin was demanding in her plan), the architect, Mario Luis Magni, at the time in the employment of the industrial complex SOMISA, conceived a plan which was agreed to by Our Lady and the eccelsiastical authorities: a large sanctuary of more than 80 meters long, dominated by a high cupola. The architect had to leave SOMISA, in order to carry out this great project.

On December 21, 1985, Our Lady insistently requested that the construction begin before the winter of 1987, which begins in June in this hemisphere. On December 21st, near the solstice, Gladys observed:

> "I have seen the plan of the santuary [completed by the architect]. Today also, when I saw Our Lady, I asked her if she liked it (she had rejected a previous plan). She smiled and told me:"
>
> — *Yes, my daughter, it is a plan which I like, for the sanctuary will be as large as I requested it. I wish then to see it become a reality, for those who will go there and pay homage to the Lord will be numerous.*
>
> *May another winter not begin without seeing that this work has started. Amen. Amen.*

We observe that the sanctuary has proportions similar to those of the Pantheon.

When winter ended in September, construction had not begun. It only started in October. And it then endured a rigorous winter of economic crisis.

Many people who had committed themselves to pay a fixed sum of money each month, could no longer provide it with the runaway inflation which reduced their incomes. The breathtaking rise in prices upset their generous predictions, while the cost of the sanctuary increased at exponential speed. Was it about this "economic winter" that the Blessed Virgin wanted to speak?

In spite of these obstacles, construction began on October 13th and by Easter, 1989, the first section was completed: first crypt, the foundation of the second, and the construction of the nave to mid height, in order to receive the pilgrims.

On Palm Sunday, March 19, 1989, the statue of Our Lady, venerated in the cathedral, was transferred to the section of the new sanctuary which was built. In his homily, Bishop Castagna stated:

> "Mysterious coincidence: we bless the first section of the sanctuary on this Palm Sunday, and we place there permanently, the holy and venerable image of 'Our Lady of the Rosary.' It is a day of joy, but not precisely one of triumph. The Church has contracted a healthy allergy against all triumphalism, which would subject it to satisfactions of a purely temporal order. In this event of God and of the Blessed Virgin, moments follow one another. Here is one among them, greatly awaited for, which permits one to foresee a future of great evangelizing activity moved by Mary (beginning of the homily of March 19. Cf. *Revista del Santuario,* #18, p. 15-16).

*CHAPTER 10*

# The Message

The message of San Nicolás is not a literary or theological work. It is words of life, words of a mother. She does not cease to repeat, for her children are slow to understand them. Those who live them understand them.

In presenting a synthesis, do we not run the risk of hardening it, impoverishing it, distorting it? One hesitates. And yet, an understanding of the faith is good. With reference to Fr. Pérez, who lives the messages and makes them lived in listening to the Bible, one sees briefly the internal logical and luminous coherence, the beauty and the love which characterize this teaching. Should it not be taken into account?

The central point (the point of convergence of more than 1800 messages given by Gladys from October 13, 1983, to February 11, 1990) focuses on this:

**GOD WANTS TO RENEW THE COVENANT WITH HIS PEOPLE, THROUGH MARY, HIS ARK OF THE COVENANT,**

for she is, according to Holy Scripture, the eschatological "Ark of the Covenant";

— The Ark of the Covenant, that is to say, the residence of God among men, and,

— eschatological, that is, of the last times. The coming of Christ in this world will begin the last phase, and will begin the final return of Christ.

## The Messages of Jesus

In San Nicolás, Gladys received 68 messages from Jesus: 1983 through 1989. Some messages were shorter, stronger. We cited the first ones in the text previously.

*He who listens to my words will find salvation. He who puts them into practice will live forever. Those who hope in God do not hope in vain.* (6/15/84, #174).

*Where you put your feet, you will step on evil. What you must do is to crush it, to eliminate it.* (6/24/84, #192).

*Never deny God. Draw nearer and listen to His call. You will not regret it.* (7/8/84, #204).

*Continue, for nothing will stop you. You have received a mission so that he who did not know the word of God may know it, and that he who carries Him in his heart may renew his love and reinforce his trust.* (7/29/84, #226).

*I speak to the poor, to the sick. God does not forget anyone.* (10/9/84, #319).

*My heart is big. It can receive every lamentation, every suffering. I am not deaf. I am not cold. My love goes as far as those who love me.* (11/11/84, #367).

*God alone knows the way, and He will show the sure path.* (11/11/84-11/19/84, #377).

*God stops before each child according to his needs, and according to the love which each feels for Him.* (12/13/84, #405).

*I do not slip away. I want to save humanity. This time, on firm ground, I am near my Arch. Blessed is he who abandons himself to God.* (2/21/85, #481).

*I know the actions of all men. I see their constancy and I verify their weaknesses. My answer depends on their actions.* (5/7/85, #550).

*If a people prays and respects my word, this people will live in peace. I will protect them.* (10/4/85, #695).

*My heart is beating. I am here like a child who is ready to be born while waiting for his delivery, in order to be able to expand in each human being.* (11/18/85, #728).

*If this generation does not listen to my mother, it will perish. I ask everyone to listen to her. Man's conversion is necessary. It is better to look up and to know what He Who is there says, rather than to move adrift. Think about it.* (3/12/86, #839).

*Under the species of the Holy Eucharist, my Heart is introduced into all open hearts. It nourishes them; it satisfies them.* (3/27/86, #839).

*My Heart takes all souls into consideration. My Heart wishes the salvation of all souls and loves them, even those who are in sin.* (6/6/86, #890).

*People always suffer from the same illness: pride. It is evil in the eyes of God and I want to correct your brothers. That spreads to the whole world. If souls lack love and faith, it is in vain that I try to reach them. Holy souls need permanent assistance from God. I will grant to holy souls consolation and mercy.* (8/16/86, #944).

"His hands shone with a white light," Gladys observed on that day.

*I place the love of my mother with all people so that they may have recourse to her. She is the help that will make Christians come out of darkness, in order to introduce them into the light. Invoke her name with an intense love.* (10/14/87, #1276).

*Today I warn the world, for the world is not aware: souls are in danger. Many are lost. Few will find salvation unless they accept me as their Savior. My mother must be accepted. My mother must be heard in the totality of her messages. The world must discover the richness which she brings to Christians. The children of sin will grow up in sin if their unbelief increases. I want a renewal of the spirit, a detachment from death, and an attachment to life. I have chosen the heart of my mother, so that what I ask will be achieved. Souls will come to me through the means of her Immaculate Heart.* (11/19/87, #1302).

*Souls are in confusion, for evil wants to invade the earth, and darkness wants to destroy everything. I will shed blessings on all those who direct their steps toward me. May those who have founded their hope on the love of God and His justice be in joy.* (2/18/88, #1355).

*What would I not do for humanity if humanity would consecrate itself to God and to prayer.* (5/12/88, #1417).

*There is no room for me in all hearts. Since this is so, I am going to expand the time. Everything has not withered. There are green stalks whence new shoots will grow.* (6/16/88, #1444).

*A cry comes from My Heart and is directed to mankind: do not be alone. Look for God. My hand is always extended.* (7/8/88, #1457).

## *The Last Messages of Jesus April 25-December 30, 1989*

*He who loves the food which I give him must know that he is well nourished. I am the food and drink of the soul, which thirsts for God. In me, the soul will be satisfied, for I am the hope which becomes life.* (4/25/89, #1646).

*My Heart and my glance are turned toward the earth, and I say to you: you will need me. I will save you. I have had mercy on those who love me.* (6/2/89, #1665).

*My creatures should come to me, because it is only near me that they will live forever. My mother will not permit them to go adrift. She will conduct them directly to me.* (7/25/89, #1685).

*So many souls do not know me. I try to find again, so many souls. If my voice meets with indifference, it is because of hardened hearts. It is time to bury unbelief. I am waiting for souls. Let them not stop.* (9/30/89, #1721).

*I feed my flock because it disturbs me very much. My Heart is burning with love, but there are hearts which are completely extinguished. They do not receive the love which I give to all souls. My light wants to illuminate all nations, for it is the true light. All those who receive it will be called true children of God.* (11/17/89, #1750).

*In the past, the world was saved by the Ark of Noah. Today my mother is the Ark. It is through her, that souls will be saved, because she will lead them to me. He who rejects my mother, rejects me. Many are those who allow the grace of God to pass these days.* (12/30/89, #1778).

Jesus said that after He had shown Gladys the work of the creation of the world; then He added:

*Go and preach the Gospel. Little does it matter where you do it. Wherever you are, preach the Gospel to your brothers who do not know the word of God. Preach the Gospel. (ibid).*

It was the last message of Jesus to Gladys, a month and 12 days before the end of the messages.

During 1984, the messages of Christ become a little more frequent. On January 3rd, He actualizes the Gospel:

*Go to the aid of the poor,*
*Go to the aid of the rich man as well as of the disinherited,*
*For they no longer have the faith.*
*Let them know my mercy.*
*I do not reject him who looks for me.*
*You should not be silent.*
*Speak and do not stop preaching.*
*I am your strength. Amen.* (1/23/84, #27).

It is indeed the Gospel, the Good News announced to the poor, which manifests itself for our concluding millennium. The rich are also the poor; *"for they no longer have the faith."* Jesus recalls His mercy. He invites Gladys to evangelization.

Other messages continued during the following months. On February 3, 1984:

*He whose heart is healthy, let him keep it healthy, and not allow himself to become contaminated. He who walks in my footsteps will inherit eternal life, and he who keeps my commandments will be my companion for the rest of his days. Let no one be frightened with my words. That is what you should say to your brothers.* (#40).

The density of the above message appears in reference to the Gospel itself:

*Blessed are the pure of heart, for they shall see God.* (*Matt.* 5:8).

*He who wishes to come after me, let him renounce himself, carry his cross each day, and follow me.* (*Matt.* 16:24).

*Blessed are those who listen to the word of God and keep it.* (*Lk.* 11:28).

*I will no longer call you servants but my friends.* (*Jn.* 15:15).

*Do not fear.* (*Lk.* 1:13, 30).

On March 6th, the fifth message from Jesus:

*May your eyes and your heart refer to your God. I want it. Woe to the man who disobeys Me. It is not worth anything to him. And he will not find anything that will replace Me. I call you my children, and I want you to be my children.* (3/6/84, #72).

On the following month, April 1984, there were two messages from Jesus. On April 1st:

*I do not remain at a distance from him who needs me. I remain by his side.*

*Pray for yourselves and pray for your brothers.* (#101).

And on the 29th:

*I will reproach the attitude of him who invokes God, then separates himself from Him. But I will have mercy on him who invokes me in all truth.* (#1324).

From that time onward the messages continued at the rate of about one a month, until December 30, 1989, for a total of 68 (the most significant are quoted on pages 42-45). Here are more of the most salient:

On January 29, 1985, Gladys wrote:

> "I see Jesus dressed in a white tunic. A brilliant light shines in the middle of His chest. He says to me:" *What you see is My Heart which is trembling in the face of hostility from the world toward God. I wish for mankind to discover salvation. This is the reason for this manifestation of love for humanity.*

And Our Lady adds:

> *Let the hours to come be devoted to the Lord. He deserves all your time. He deserves all of your attention as well as your thanksgiving because His ear is sensitive to your prayers. Amen. Amen.*

On March 28, 1985, Jesus resumes the same confidence by adding:

> *My Heart is deep and all those who give themselves to me with trust will be able to enter it.*

And the Blessed Virgin observes:

> *My dear children, I assure you that you will not be far from my dear Son, if you succeed in trusting in Him [. . .].*
>
> *He wants to remove us from adversity, and He offers you everlasting life. Amen. Amen!*

It is a message of love and of mercy. On May 28, 1985, Jesus said:

> *I, the heir of love of My Father, pour out this love in the world so that it may return to its point of departure: to my most Holy Father.* (#570).

It is the great cycle of love which Jesus wants to establish. It flows from the Love of the Trinity and returns to it forever.

The symbolic vision of July 21, 1984, summarizes everything pictorially. Gladys states:

> "I see some fire. I do not know what is burning, but there is much fire. Then there is very much water which puts out the fire. The Blessed Virgin tells me:"
>
> *The water which you see is the strength of God which drives away the Evil One, for he wants to destroy what one has so much difficulty in obtaining—faith in God and love of God. Glory be to God forever.*

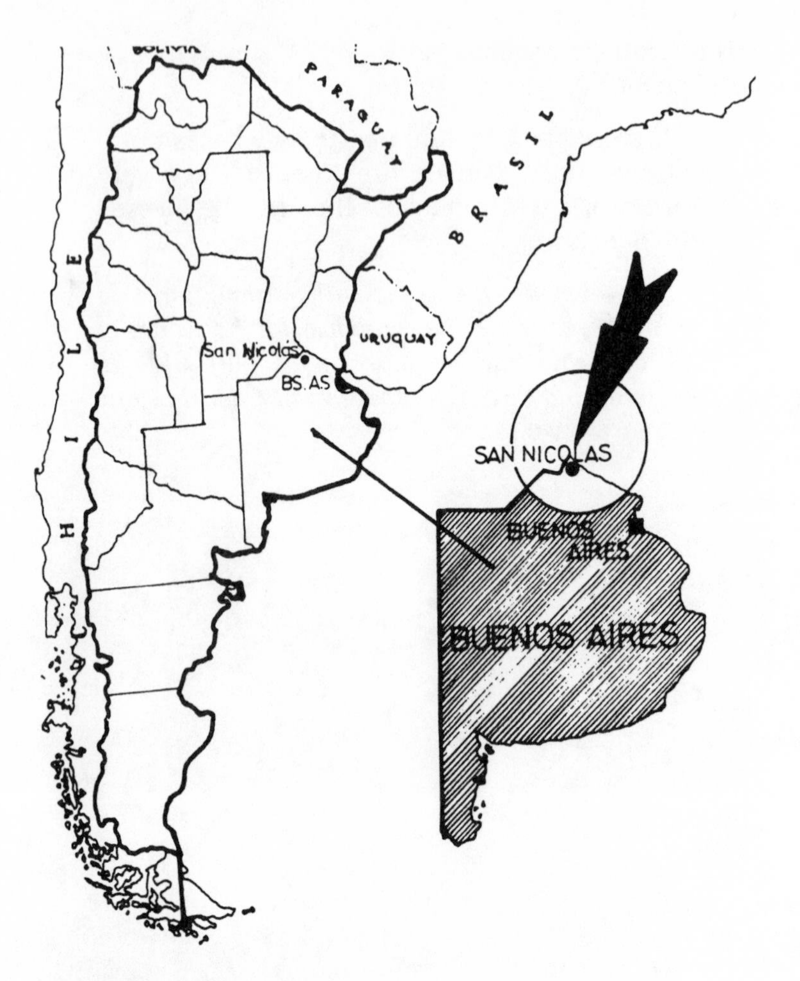


***ARGENTINA***

AREA: Over 1,000,000 square miles

POPULATION: Over 24,000,000

CAPITAL: Buenos Aires

LOCATION: The southern half of South America on the Atlantic coast.

**Sr. Maria Crescencia Pérez (1897-1932)**

## *Relationship Between San Nicolás and Pergamino*

On page 29, we gave details of the cure of a young boy from Pergamino, Gonzalo Miguel Godoy. Father Busso, Chancelar of the Bishopric, had prepared him for his first Holy Communion when he was at the point of death. Father Busso was also a native of Pergamino, and was a friend of the family, having baptized all of the Godoy children.

Fr. Pérez, rector of the new Sanctuary, and also a native of Pergamino, had an aunt who was a religious there. Sr. Maria Crescencia was a nun with the Sisters of Our Lady of the Garden, in Pergamino. She died in the odor of sanctity at the age of 34, closely affiliated with San Nicolás. It is another stage in the history of San Nicolás where so many pre-destined children come together. Sr. Maria had a great love for the Sacred Heart, the Cross and Mary. In one of her letters, July 20, 1924, she said:

> "Every day I ask the good Lord and our Mother of the Garden (del huerto), to bless and advise us for all those whom they wish to submit to the Sisters of the Garden through our works and sufferings, for as long as we are here below, we necessarily have to suffer and struggle. For that it is necessary for us to raise our eyes to Heaven and to implore the strength which is needed."

She had a great love of the child Jesus in His Incarnation. She derived a profound meaning from it. It shows in the record of her service to the people, every day of her life.

*Basilica Construction, 1988.*

*Basilica Construction, 1988.*

*Model of the new Basilica Sanctuary being constructed in San Nicolás.*

*"Our Lady of the Rosary" statue in the original Cathedral.*

*Msgr. Castagna,
Bishop of San Nicolás.*

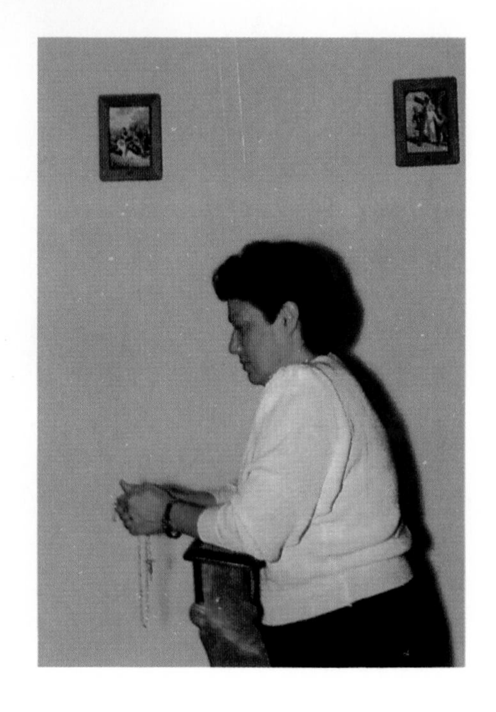

*Gladys, the seer,
during prayer.*

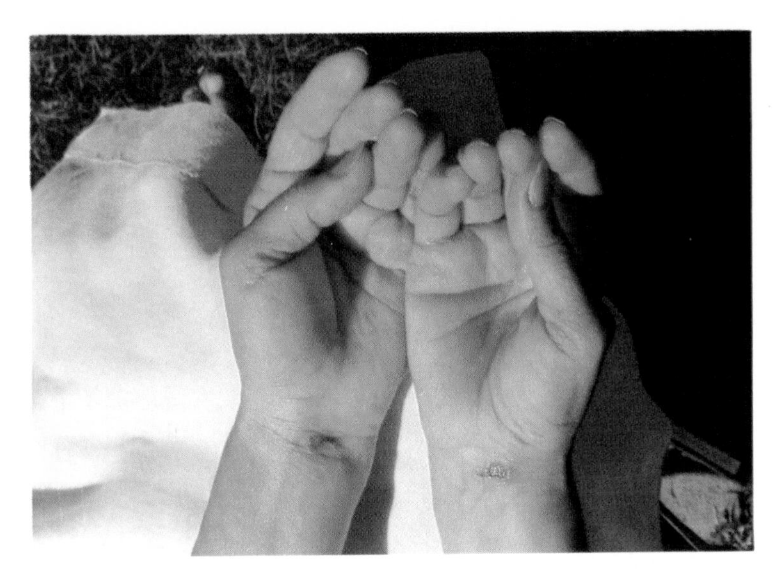

*The stigmata of the wrists of Gladys (observe the position of the thumbs).*

*"Our Lady of the Rosary" in the Cathedral.*

*Gonzalo,*
*cured by Our Lady.*

*The devotions are led by the Bishop of San Nicolás.*

*The procession on the 25th of each month.*

*THE MESSAGE—PART 1*

# Mary, Mother And Ark Of The Covenant

## *A Key Reference: Revelation* 11-12

The key to the messages is found in *Revelation* 11:19 and 12:1-17. Mary appears in Heaven under two successive and juxtaposed forms:

— First of all, as Ark of the Covenant (11:19—the last verse of the chapter)
— Then (without transition) as the woman clothed with the Sun (12:1), Mother of the Messiah (12:2-5) and of all the people—"her offspring" (12:17); all of that in a terrible struggle against the demon where she stands by her Son, the Messiah, and her other children, the disciples (cf. *Jn.* 19:25-27), where the dying Jesus entrusts to Mary this maternal task.

First of all, let us read the biblical text again:

*In Heaven, the sanctuary of God opens and the Ark of the Covenant appears in this sanctuary [. . .].*
*Then a great sign appeared in Heaven: a woman clothed with the sun, the moon under her feet. On her head a crown of 12 stars. She was with child and she moaned with the pains of childbirth.* (cf. *Is.* 66:7).
*Then another sign appeared in Heaven: a large red dragon with seven heads and ten horns [. . .], and his tail dragged a third of the stars from Heaven*

*and hurled them on the earth and the dragon stood before the woman who was about to give birth in order to devour her child when she would give birth. And she gave birth to a son, a male, who must rule all nations with an iron scepter* (*Ps.* 29). *Her Child was taken to God and to His throne (Ascension) and the woman fled to the desert [. . .]. There was a war in Heaven: Michael and his angels waged war against the dragon and his angels with him.* (*Apoc.* 11:19-12:7).

The message of San Nicolás mentions this struggle on September 29, 1989, on the Feast of the Holy Archangels:

"I had a vision," observed Gladys, "that three white lights, equal in grandeur and intensity, descended upon me. And the Blessed Virgin is in the midst of a still greater white light.

"She said to me:"

*My daughter, today you have the special protection of the archangels. They fight intrepidly against evil under all its forms as messengers of God, [. . .].*

*They defend the soul against the perils of the devil. They open a breach of light for the soul in the midst of darkness. They restore health of body and prepare the soul with a more intense desire for salvation according to the spirit.* (#1732).

The Apocalypse continues (12:13-17):

*When the dragon was hurled to the earth, he pursued the woman who had given birth to the male child. And the two wings of the large eagle were given to the woman in order to fly away to the desert, to her place [. . .], far from the face of the serpent. And the serpent ejected from its mouth, behind the woman, water as a river in order to carry her by the river but the earth came to the assistance of the woman and the earth opened its mouth and engulfed the river which the dragon*

> *had ejected from its mouth. And the dragon became furious against the woman and went to wage war against the rest of her offspring: those who keep the commandments of God and possess the testimony of Jesus.* (*Apoc.* 12:8-17).

Let us understand the series of events. Mary appears successfully as "Ark of the Covenant," then as the "Woman," mother of the Messiah, King of the Unvierse, but in conflict with the dragon. The labor pains are not directed at the birth of Christmas (transcendant prototype of childbirth without pains), but the painful childbirth of the Passion, as A. Feuillet has well demonstrated. "It is the tragic moment when Mary, while losing her Son by death, becomes mother of the disciples (*Jn.* 19:25-27)." (A. Feuillet, *Jesus et sa Mere,* Paris, Gabalda, 1974, p. 141).

When her Son ascended into Heaven (Ascension), Mary remained on earth. She will continue to visit it, for she strengthens the Church. She is the Church, as a message of San Nicolás (#1129) says. She participates in the struggles—the struggles of her children, the disciples of Christ, mentioned in the last verse (*Apoc.* 12:17 and *Jn.* 19:25-27).

The messages of San Nicolás present Mary very explicitly as the woman of *Apocalypse* 12:

> *The Lord has marked this time with a sign: the woman clothed with the sun. She represents the hope to which her children must cling.* (2/28/89, #1616).

She also appeared as the mother of her children in distress, and she looks upon them with love. The message continues:

> *The Mother has looked upon you. It is up to you to put your eyes and your heart on God, so that all forms of glory be given to Him.* (ibid).

Before saying these explanatory words, Mary had appeared to Gladys, silently and radiantly, as "the woman clothed with the Sun," Who is Christ, Son of justice. In this manner she had already appeared in 1531 in Guadalupe, then in 1830 on the rue du Bac, and in Lourdes in 1858. Her light (that of God) preceded the apparition and disappeared after it. "The Light was God," said the visionaries in Fatima.

## *Mary Involved In the Covenant*

But before saying how the mother of Christ is also the Ark of the Covenant of which the Apocalypse speaks, let us look at the substance of the matter. The condition of our world, forgetful of God and abandoned to sin, is an acknowledgment of failure.

After the struggles of the Old Testament, God established a new covenant with and through Mary. Through her and with her, He brought about His Incarnation, and He wanted her presence at the foot of the Cross, at the cruel hour of the Redemption, when He entrusted to her, her mission as mother of the disciples.

Today this covenant is broken in our world, deliberately desecrated, secularized, materialized. It seems God no longer has His place in it, because the "practical" materialism of free countries is at times more ingratiating, anesthetizing, or perverse, than the "ideological" materialism of the countries of the East.

This loss of love and respect for God is the source of divisions, degradations, disintegrations, and conflicts, rooted in sin.

## *A Broken Covenant*

The rebellions which I see throughout the world are atrocious. I am filled with compassion for all those who have moved away from God.

> *They lack love because they reject Him. Their sins increase from day to day. They desire them and commit them.* (1/19/85, #445).

Yes, our world has moved away from God. It mocks Him, or ignores Him. Statistics confirm it. In 1900 there were 225,000 atheists; today there are 262 million, considerably a thousand times more. Agnostics were hardly 3 million at the beginning of the century. Today they are more than a billion. These are the fruits of the culture which is strictly scientific, technical, materialistic, secularized, and which has lost its *sacred aura* (#788), and where God and man are marginal.

> *In the large cities of the world, atheism and a complete indifference toward God reign. The evil one is rising in a turmoil; his wickedness hides and controls weak souls. The Lord wants to alert us.* (9/2/85, #656).

The consequences are grave:

> *Men are in the process of falling. Their self-destruction progresses.* (2/28/89, #1616).

## *Abandoned Youth*

Our youth, poorly educated in this pernicious environment, suffer in a particular way, and Mary as Mother, is very concerned about it, beginning with "little children."

> *Pray, my daughter, for all the little children of the world; for those who do not have bread, for those who lack love, and especially for those who do not receive the Word of God.*
>
> *[. . .] He who is compassionate toward a child, is compassionate toward God. He who gives his love to a child, gives it to God. He who makes the Word of God known to a child is truly a son of God.* (8/7/88, #1481).

She worries in a maternal way, even more insistently, about the youth in peril:

*My daughter, I see the youth adrift. The devil corners them and leads them to sin. My children are harassed by evil, and the disorder of their spirits is complete. To all of them, I say to thank the Lord because of His patience, and to ask Him for His protection. Read Ecclesiastes 17:25-26.* (12/12/84, #405).

*My dear children, the young find themselves facing a corrupt, horrifying world [. . .]. Do not allow yourselves to be taken in by calamities which you have before your eyes. Do not forget that they lead to perdition by subjecting you to evil. Pray, so that you can become a youth dedicated to the Lord; a youth which is looking for peace. May this novena then, be dedicated to all the young people, and you will confirm that the Lord does not reject the children who look for Him. Read Matthew 18:6-7.* (5/8/85, #551).

*Parents, during this novena recommend yourselves to the Lord insistently, so that He may be able to shed light for your children in their own journey in this life [. . .]. You are responsible for their steps. You must lead them to the Lord so that they may say: "God is our beginning and we turn to Him."* (11/9/85, #718).

Youth is a constant concern in the messages. On December 14, 1985, it was Jesus Who said:

*Youth are in a permanent imbalance and it risks the danger of a total collapse. The majority do not build on truth for failure to know justice. They do not love God. The young people of this world must know that God does not impose anything. God wishes to stay among them. There is a dawn which is waiting. There is a door through which those who are invited by My Father, the chosen ones of My Father, are going to pass.* (12/14/85, #753).

On the following June 7th, it is Mary who speaks:

*I ask the young people of the whole world, those who have borrowed evil ways: Why do you do then so many foolish things? Are you orphans? Do you not have a God? Do you not have your heavenly Mother? It is time to purify yourselves, my dear children! How many lamentations later, if you do not do it! Read Isaiah 45:22-24.* (6/7/86, #891).

And she returns incessantly to it (as, incidentally, in Medjugorje):

*Youth is sadly running to its perdition, the easy life and drugs. Such is the panorama which the evil one uses in facing young people. A whole gamut of a variety of sins separates them from God more and more. It would only be necessary for them to look toward the Mother of God, their Mother, and she would lead them to God. It would be necessary for them to introduce themselves into the heart of the Mother, in order to listen to the voice of the Lord. I do not hide myself; let no one avoid me!* (9/21/87, #1262).

*My daughter, pray for the young people of the whole world. They need divine help, for a mortal danger is threatening them. Subjection to drugs is truly a very grave danger for the youth. At this moment so many young people become slaves of Satan in the most cruel manner. The Lord does not want any more slaves and seduced beings. He wants souls who believe in eternal life and in Jesus Christ, the Savior of souls.* (6/14/88, #1441).

*Drugs are a great danger for young people. They lead them to live in the most complete immorality. Ignorance of God makes them subject themselves to darkness. That is why they must be more the children who know the Gospel, wishing to be saved by the Savior, Jesus Christ. Salvation must be widely preached; it is necessary.* (9/17/89, #1709).

For all these intentions which Mary carries in her heart as a mother, San Nicolás is a place of mercy.

## General Contamination

In one of the first messages she stated:

> *All of humanity is contaminated.* (12/27/83, #14).

Mary perceived this danger for her children, those deprived of the holiness of God:

> *At this moment, humanity is hanging by a thread. If this thread is released, many are those who will not be able to save themselves. That is why I ask you to reflect. Do not delay, for time begins to end, and there will be no more room for him who will be late.* (1/8/84, #18).

But "God wants all men to be saved." (*1 Tim.* 2:4). He confirms these words of Holy Scripture through a message at San Nicolás:

> *The Lord wants all to be able to enter into His Kingdom. Here then is what I say to all who have moved away from Him:*
> *Come, draw near, for Jesus Christ is within your reach. Amen!*
> *Announce Him! Read Hebrews 4:12-16.* (1/8/84, #18).

This scriptural text concludes:

> *Move ahead with assurance, towards the throne of glory, to receive mercy and to find the grace of opportune help.*

Mary announces Christ's return. She invites us to prepare for it. (3/26/88, #1382).

> *The coming of the Savior is imminent. As the Gospel says, no one knows the date nor the hour, but the hour will come, and it is certain that the soul of the Christian must be prepared for that*

*hour. Even the stones will be witnesses to it. That is why, my daughter, the Mother* (Mary) *wants to make known the Word of her Son.*

What is one to say? Except that the apparitions are a stage towards this eschatological return. They are a (kairos): a key moment which one must seize.

*The hour of the Mother has arrived. My heart of a mother has already begun to prepare the hearts and to act on them. I come from Heaven in order to lead you to Christ. Make it known.* (5/5/88, #1410).

## Mary, Eschatological Ark of the Covenant

The broken covenant must be reestablished. Mary was sent for that. She was completely destined for this mission, for she is the new Ark of the Covenant, according to the New Testament (*Lk.* 1:35, 39-56) and the Fathers of the Church. *Apocalypse* 11:19 and 12:19 attest to the same identification.

*Then there appeared in the heavens the Ark of the Covenant of God.* (*Apoc.* 11:19).

What does this mean?

The Ark is the sign of the first covenant. Moses who guided the Hebrews in the desert during the Exodus, had it constructed (*Ex.* 25 and 40), in order to be the residence of God in the midst of His people, for God had come to live in it:

*The* (radiant) *cloud covered the meeting tent* (which contained the Ark of the Covenant) *And the glory of Yahweh filled the dwelling.* (*Ex.* 30:24).

The cloud above signified the transcendence of the inaccessible God, and the radiant glory inside signified His immanence, familiarity, communication: in brief, His alliance with His people.

Moses then placed it under a tent, analogous to that of the wandering people. It reminded them that men need God and that God is with them.

The wooden Ark was a figure. It was fulfilled in Mary, who became (after the disappearance of the Ark at the time of the exile in Babylonia), the new dwelling of God-made-man for a new Covenant—the Covenant of the last times. She thus became "the Ark of the Living Covenant," stated the Fathers of the Church. For the Ark of Moses was only an inert and unconscious piece of wooden furniture. Mary is a person, who receives God in a holy manner and as a very loving mother, for the Son of God became her Son.

The angel of the Annunciation identifies to her, her mission of eschatological Ark of the Covenant in taking up, literally, the words of *Exodus* on the coming of God in the old Ark of the Covenant:

> *The Holy Spirit will come upon you, and the power of the Most High will overshadow you.*
> *That is why He Who will be born* (of you), *will be called Holy, Son of God.* (*Lk.* 1:35, where one find the words of *Ex.* 40:35).

As in the desert, God comes above (transcendence) and within (immanence). But at the Annunciation, this immanence is the Incarnation of God among mankind. The radiant glory that shone from the primitive Ark is duplicated by the humble and discreet presence of the Son of God, conceived by the Holy Spirit, humanly formed in Mary.

It was not an unforeseen event. For centuries, the prophets (*Soph.* 3, more specifically) announced a new Ark of the Covenant for the last times. And this new residence of God was no longer a piece of furniture but a living person, a woman—the daughter of Zion, ideal personalization of the people of God. It did not deal with a purely symbolical personification, but a real personalization, for

Mary fulfills the perfection of the people slowly educated by God, and her grace begins that of the Holy Church, which is recommended to us all.

The woman, mysteriously announced by the prophets then, was Mary. And the angel Gabriel takes up the words of Sophonias in order to announce to her, the coming of the Son of God in her womb. Here is the comparison of the texts:

| *Old Testament* | *New Testament* |
|---|---|
| Annunciation of the...... | Annunciation of the |
| prophet to Israel......... | angel to Mary |
| (*Soph.* 3:14-17).......... | (*Lk.* 1:28-33) |
| 14. Rejoice, you......... | 28. Rejoice, you |
| Daughter of Zion........ | Full of grace |
| 15ab. Yahweh King of..... | the Lord |
| Israel is in your midst..... | is in your womb |
| 16. Do not fear, Zion...... | 30. Do not fear, Mary |
| 17. Yahweh your God..... | 31. Behold, you will |
| in your midst........... | conceive in your womb |
| ........................ | and you will bring forth a |
| ........................ | Son and you will give |
| ........................ | Him a name |
| 17. Lord thy God is mighty. | 32. Yahweh the Savior |
| ........................ | (=Jesus) |
| He will save............ | 33. He will reign without |
| ........................ | end. |

Indeed then, Mary is the living Ark of the Covenant which gives birth to God in His people, an extraordinary and new marvel: *"the Word became flesh and He dwelt among us,"* summarized St. John the Apostle, a relative of Mary. (*Jn.* 1:14). And the word "dwell" (Greek: *eskenosen*), is the same one which the Old Testament used to define the dwelling place of God in the Ark of the Covenant.

The account of the Visitation (*Lk.* 1:39-56) takes up this typology again, always through the use of biblical and prophetic terms of the Old Testament. Luke inculcates this same identification. He narrates the visit of Mary to Elizabeth while profiling the account of the transfer of the Ark—when David led it back to Jerusalem (according to *Samuel* 6:1-23). It thus stressed that Mary accomplished in fullness, the mystery of the Ark of the Covenant, and the Ascent of God to His Holy City (R. Laurentin, *Les Evangiles de Noel, Paris, Desclee, 1985, p. 86-88).*

In San Nicolás Jesus Himself presents, "His Ark," Mary, in the vision of February 21, 1985. (#481). He tells Gladys:

> *I do not hide myself. I want to save humanity. This time, on firm ground, I am near my Ark. Blessed is he who abandons himself to God.*

The coming of Mary to San Nicolás established a place of grace, a new Jerusalem, City of God in the Promised Land:

> "I see the Blessed Virgin and behind her there appears a great light. It is as if a mountain would open and within it one sees a valley illuminated also by that light."
>
> *Child, it is the horizon of the Lord; in it I want all my children to enter. I call them all alike. I also want to be heard. I also want to feel the joy of being understood as every mother who wants the best for her children. Amen. Amen!* (12/29/84, #427).

Will we understand the Mystery of this Presence? (*Shekinah* according to the Bible?) Mary is its founding place.

> *Only a mean heart can doubt the Presence of God in this place. Only a poor soul will not be able to understand that the Ark is here and that there is sufficient room for those who want to enter into it. The Lord stopped me here, so that from here I may call my children and receive them. Amen. Amen!* (4/17/85, #531).

## ***The Ark and the Anchor***

Mary, faithful to her mission of new Ark of the Covenant, comes then to the banks of the Paraná in order to restore the house of God in His people. Gladys has a vision of it:

> "I see a river; I think that it is ours, and a large canoe. It looks like an ark. The Virgin Mary tells me:" *I am the anchor. I have anchored here. I am the Ark and I want to lead my children to the Lord.* (10/14/84, #327).

Here, the image is no longer that of the ark of Moses, carried on the back of men, but the ark of Noah; that ship which saved life from the waves of the deluge. The last message of Christ explains it:

> *Formerly, the world was saved by the ark of Noah. Today the ark is my mother. Through her, souls will be saved because she will lead them to me.* (12/30/89, #1778).

Mary came to the banks of the Paraná in order to establish herself "on firm ground" as the message of Jesus, dated February 21, 1985 (#481), already taught.

Our Lady has cast anchor, not on the marshy islands of the large river, but on the firm bank where the people live. A ray of light showed the building site of the future basilica. It is not then a ship that one wants to construct, but a church of stone. And the church, house of God, is the symbol of the Blessed Virgin Mary, for it is in her that God established His dwelling when He came into this world. That is why the first large Christian churches were dedicated to Our Lady.

The anchor is what holds the ship against winds and tides. The Blessed Virgin came to settle in San Nicolás. The sanctuary where she receives us will be her irresistible anchor, the place which she has chosen and designated by a ray of light.

The day when they laid the first stone, "the cornerstone" of the sanctuary, the Blessed Virgin told Gladys:

> *My daughter of predilection, for three years I have continuously watched and I draw nearer to all my children. Receive from the Lord His blessing on this day. With this cornerstone, the mother of Christ remains from today and always, anchored here next to her dear children in this holy land. Glory to God forever.* (9/25/86, #976).

Those who present the ark according to biblical archeology—a wooden box carried on the backs of men—will be astonished that the Blessed Virgin says: *I cast anchor in San Nicolás.* Why this maritime symbol? The fact is that Mary compares her coming on the banks of the Paraná to the docking of a ship—a beautiful symbol of the Church and of her, for "Mary is the Church" according to the message of March 18, 1987. (#1129).

On October 12, 1984, Gladys observed again:

> "I see an anchor and along its side a fish, and some bread. The anchor is blue." (#324).

Two days later the Blessed Virgin spoke clearly:

> *It is I who am the anchor. I have anchored here.* (10/14/84, #327).

The sanctuary of Mary, new Ark of the Covenant, built in San Nicolás is the place of her teaching. She invites us to remain with her and in her for our spiritual formation, as Jesus remained there for His human formation. (#881, 1427).

*THE MESSAGE—PART 2*

# The Signs Of Mary

The woman of the Apocalypse, from whom God has made His Ark of the Covenant, manifests herself to her children through simple, popular signs which are rooted in the lives of the people:

— The traditional statue of "Our Lady of the Rosary," which was in the cathedral.
— The sanctuary, which Mary invited to be built as place and symbol of her presence.
— The medal which she asked Gladys to have made.

## *1. The Statue*

First of all, it is the statue of "Our Lady of the Rosary," to whom the people had entrusted themselves long ago: first in Rosario (the founding bishop, today an archbishop), and then in San Nicolás itself, where Our Lady of the Rosary had settled a century ago. Mary recalls from the first messages:

> *I will settle in the midst of you* (message of November 27, 1983, Feast of the Miraculous Medal and first day of the novena to San Nicolás (Pérez #19); likewise on November 24 (Pérez #15): *It is my place.*

That same November 27th, Father Pérez called Gladys to view the traditional statue, which he found with a broken hand in the belfry. Gladys recognized it and Our Lady confirmed it. She appeared, living and radiant, before the statue, and said:

> *They had kept me in oblivion, but I rose again. Set me for you see me such as I am. Do not be concerned, you will have me. I want to be on the bank of the Paraná; the place which I chose.* (11/27/83, Pérez #20).

The statue of the "Queen of the Rosary," which presided over the destinies of San Nicolás, had been forgotten, relegated. The Blessed Virgin honored this sign of her presence. And her return was celebrated by huge crowds. The statue, borne shoulder high as previously the Ark of the Covenant was, seemed to sail on these crowds as on an ocean of love. Thus Mary found her place again and the forgotten role which her people had formerly given her.

## 2. The Sanctuary

She also asked for a new sanctuary which will be a new sign of her presence. The Christian churches, inhabited by the Blessed Sacrament, are the new Ark of the Covenant. And Mary, in whom Christ came to dwell in body, founded this mystery of the new alliance. Thus, since that time, every church (House of God) is perceived as a symbol of Mary.

So you see why the construction of a new sanctuary dedicated to Mary on the banks of the Paraná holds such a place in the message. The symbol (the sanctuary), and the reality (Mary), which is also the Church, according to the Council and the message of San Nicolás, are inseparable. Mary formally identifies the construction of her sanctuary, and the building of the Body of Christ, which have the same objective.

She urges the construction of this sanctuary where grace already abounds:

> *You must ask with firmness; give importance to my petition. My house has to be built, my children. Give your mother what she asks you. Invite people to pray at the place which has been chosen and sanctified by me. And my children will come.* (11/23/84, #383).

On December 5, 1984, Our Lady made this request in almost the same words:

> *It is necessary to build my house and to give your mother what she asks. If you invite my children here, at this place which I have chosen and sanctified so that they may pray, they will come.* (12/5/84, #398).

On December 18th, she repeated it at the place chosen and blessed by her:

> *I hope to be able to receive you soon in the house which I have chosen.* (#414).

Here, she invites Gladys to read *Tobit* 13:10-13, which identifies all its meaning, if one understands that Jerusalem is also Mary and the church which she asks to be built.

On December 27th, Our Lady stated that her house would also be the house of the people who built it:

> *My house will be your house, this place of peace which every good Christian needs. It will be like a harbor of calm waters, where you will be able to permeate with the love of God. Amen. Amen!* (#425).

The symbolics of Our Lady combines earth and water, the rock of the Church, and the fountain of grace which springs from it.

On February 2, 1985, she insisted again, but in thanksgiving:

*Blessed be the moment when the Lord chose this people and blessed be He because He has chosen it so that it may build my large house. This house will be a house of peace and of rest; the place where I will rock to sleep the thousands of children who will come in search of love. I am going to attend the sick there, the sinners, and every child belonging to the large family of God, because my mission is to concern myself with the whole flock of the Lord. Glory to God!* (2/2/85, #463).

She rejoiced on the day when Bishop Castagna laid the foundation stone. (9/25/86, #976).

On October 14, 1987, she encouraged the work in progress. She accompanied and protected it. (#1277).

On October 20, 1987, she clearly stated the purpose of the sanctuary: "it will gather together her children and it will be the place of their purification for the salvation of the world. It will be the place of her presence."

*You will not see me but my heart will beat with love toward my beloved children.* (10/20/87, #1281).

This sanctuary *will make the work of God grow. It will be an armor for the people,* she added on April 9, 1988. (#1391).

She insisted on this protection on April 12, 1988:

*Nothing will be able to extinguish the flame of love which the Lord has lighted there. Nothing will be able to obscure the light of the Lord.* (#1395).

On April 22, 1988, she refers the sanctuary to her Son:

*This sanctuary, home of the Mother, is for her children. [. . .] It is the place where the mother gathers them together in order to let them meet her Son. It is the place where her Son, through the mercy of the Father, offers Himself in the Holy*

*Eucharist: deep communication between God and man, and the very powerful love of God toward man and for man.* (#1400).

It is in this sanctuary that Mary, Mother of Christ, awaits the children whom she has inherited at the foot of the Cross. It is in this sanctuary that Mary acts in souls for the benefit of souls.

On Palm Sunday, 1989, when the first section of the temple was dedicated, they brought her statue there. She greeted thus the new stage:

*Dearest children, you see it. Here I am before you. While some live in their own desolation, others will live in the house of the Mother of the Savior. This is the temple of the people of God. Here the love of Christ and of Mary will be rooted more profoundly.*

*My house will be the dwelling of those who regard themselves as children of God.*

*Rejoice, for I will bless you from here. Alleluia!* (3/19/89, #1626).

On October 7, 1989 (#1728), Gladys sees the completed construction beforehand.

"I have a vision. I see the sanctuary completed. And I see then the Blessed Virgin who tells me:"

*My daughter, the temple is protection of God for His children. They will hasten there in order to worship the Lord and to ask for physical help and a strong spirit cemented by faith. The temple is the protection of God for the soul who lives on earth and lives in Heaven.* (10/7/89, #1728).

And here she clarifies the meaning of temple: place of residence and symbol of the people of God, formed by living stones:

> *I ask for its completion. The material construction means the spiritual reconstruction of souls for the Lord.* (ibid).

The sanctuary which Our Lady requests is also the moving sign of construction of the spiritual temple, which is the people of God, the Mystical Body of Christ.

Mary, dwelling place of God and model of the Church, establishes thus in San Nicolás, the new Jerusalem, of which she is the symbol and the model:

> *Your city is the city of Mary, and it will always be a meeting place with Jesus and with His mother. Let no one intervene in my path. If someone wants to follow the Lord, let him follow me. Amen, Amen!* (9/26/85, #682).

## 3. The Medal

A third more intimate sign is the medal which Our Lady asked Gladys to strike, on December 2, 1984:

> *You must strike a medal with my image and my words: 'Mary of the Rosary of San Nicolás,' and on the reverse side the Holy Trinity with seven stars.* (#394bis: placed out of date, after #880).

We know this medal which today has been widely distributed:

— On one side, the image of Mary with the title which expresses her bond to San Nicolás.

— On the other, a triangle, a symbol of the Trinity, surrounded by seven stars. The Blessed Virgin stated on September 25, 1985 (second anniversary of the first apparition):

> *My daughter, I am going to tell you the meaning of the seven stars. These are seven graces which*

> *my Son Jesus Christ is going to grant those who wear it on their chest.* (#681bis: placed out of date, after #880).

A medal is a memorial, a pledge, a bond with what it represents, Mary and God Himself.

*THE MESSAGE—PART 3*

# Purpose And Struggle

## *Restoration of the Faith*

First of all, Mary comes to restore the faith:

— *My daughter, I have already told you, that from here faith in Jesus and in Mary will be born again.*
— *From here, I invite the world to look for the living fountain, the source of peace, the fountain of grace.* (1/26/86, #788).

She also comes to heal:

— *I want to heal my children from this sickness, which is materialism: a sickness which makes many children suffer. I want to help them to discover Christ, and I want to let them know that Christ prevails over everything.* (ibid).

Our Lady had difficulty making this message understood, but in San Nicolás, the reception was good:

— *Everywhere in the world where my messages have been given, it would seem that one preached in the cemeteries. The response which the Lord expected was not there. That is why your people were chosen. Preach, so that your brothers may answer the call of the Lord Our God.* (2/18/84, #55).
— *This city has grown in the faith, but it has to grow even more. It must be a model for Christianity.* (10/13/84, #325).

— *This country still keeps itself almost intact compared with other countries which have spiritually deteriorated, almost destroyed.*
— *In those places the mind of man, for the most part, is dominated by the evil one; here, just the opposite happens. The fact is that the work of God is bearing its fruits. In this country my children are entrusting themselves to the Lord, and evil never enters where God dwells.* (2/14/86, #801).

## Spiritual Struggle

All of that will not come about without a great struggle.

— *All of humanity is contaminated. It does not know what it wants and it is the opportunity of the evil one, but he will not come forth triumphant. Christ Jesus will win the great battle, my child [. . .]. You must not let yourself be surprised; be on your guard.* (12/27/83, #14).
— *Repeatedly they strike my heart; I feel it so, each time that Christ Jesus is offended.*
*The enemy is mercilessly challenging me; he is tempting my children openly. It is a struggle between the light and darkness, a constant persecution of my beloved Church.* (5/22/86, #881).

## The Devil

The woman of the Apocalypse recalls the dramatic struggle with the devil (the dragon), about which *Genesis* 3:15 already spoke:

> *I will place an enmity between your seed and her seed. You will strike at His heel and He will crush your head.*

*Apocalypse* 12 refers to this same woman and to this same dramatic struggle.

In San Nicolás, Mary often recalls this combat: hers, that of her Son, and that of her children, inseparably.

*Many times you will feel threatened, but do not be afraid. It is only that; only threats. Your mother tells you: never doubt in the things of the Lord.* (7/23/84, #220).

*You are continuously attacked by the evil one*[1]*, but you will reject everything. Only in this manner will he lose his strength and will he be destroyed. Be prudent and he will not destroy you; you will find strength in the Lord.* (10/10/84, #321).

*The great strength of God breaks every plan which the enemy wants to prepare. The evil one is stepped upon and dragged by the total will of the Lord. In you, you must desire it so that it may happen this way.* (11/3/84, #358).

On the morning of February 5, 1985, Gladys had this frightful "vision":

> "I was standing facing a street where enormous monsters came in my direction like an avalanche. They were horrible. Some appeared like dinosaurs and others were frightful human beings with huge heads and ears. When they were very near me, a blue wall appeared, and came between the monsters and me."

Strange vision of horror. It has its meaning. For the tempter introduces himself under enticing outward appearances as a seducer which offers pleasures, paradisiac drugs, power, fortune, and glory. Our Lady exposed its hideous reality. . .which one often discovers very late, at the end of the seduction (the fall of Hitler after his triumphs). Mary comments thus on this vision:

*These monsters represent the evil one, who wants to attack the Church, and the wall is my protecting*

---

1. Gladys writes "the evil one" with a small "e" even though the Blessed Virgin tells her to write the name of important things with a capital letter.

*mantle. It is the Lord Who makes me responsible for protecting you. My dear children, I am going to defend you.* (2/5/85, #467).

*I want to snatch them out of this subjugating force, which drags them to perdition. That force is going to cancel itself out soon. It is going to die. It has already disappeared for many of you, for you have listened to the voice of the Lord. Place yourselves in His hands. Do not permit your life to be snatched from you. Read 1 Corinthians* 6:18 *and 1 Peter* 5:8. (2/18/85, #478).

It is about a serious combat, and morbid passions have blinded many people.

*Sin exceeds all measure. The devil wants to have complete dominion over the earth; he wants to destroy. But the Lord does not want conquered ones, but conquerors. Definitely conquer the evil which surrounds you. Victory is in God. Read Apocalypse* 21:6-8. (6/2/85, #575).

On September 11, 1985, a new vision: there were frightful animals of a red and black color. They were marked with the word "ABADDON," which means the father of evil. The Blessed Virgin told her:

*If the devil acts ferociously, do not be scared. He attacks without compassion, involving whatever he can touch. Pray, because prayer strengthens. You are called by Jesus Christ to pray.* (9/11/85, #666).

On March 7, 1986, a new vision of "crawling serpents with large blind eyes, trapped in a light green fog as though asphyxiated." The Blessed Virgin explained:

*The prince of evil knows that his sad kingdom is coming to an end. In this way, he sheds his poison with all his strength. There is only a little left. His end is approaching. Amen.* (3/7/86, #817).

*The evil one [. . .] is astute and calculating. He wants to destroy, but here he will not be able to do it. Here, it is he who will self-destruct.* (3/17/86, #826).

Victory and hope dominate these messages:

*Let no one be condemned, and let everyone look for strength in the Lord. That is what your mother wants since human weaknesses are strengthened only in God.* (4/3/86, #846).

*God gives complete freedom and He allows each one the care to make his own choice: to purify oneself or to live in sin, grow in Christ or be annihilated. I advise my children to stay away from the somber night, for the dawn is going to appear soon. While you wait, let yourselves be prepared by this mother. Introduce your hearts into the Ark which Jesus has sent. Read Galatians* 4:3-11. (5/22/86, #881).

*There is darkness everywhere and the distractions, which always spread. It is the evil one and his apparent victory. But the work of God will be accomplished. God's justice will save the just.* (7/23/86, #926).

*Today, so many souls are victims of Satan. They have moved away from God and they do not look for His help. [. . .] The soul must fortify itself with the strength from God. The proud dominate the abyss and will dominate it always.* (3/22/88, #1378).

Our Lady invites us to open our eyes:

*Gladys, today, those who are dangerously seduced by the evil one are many. I ask my children: do you not see that darkness is in front of you? Do you not see that it is surrounding you? Do not be victims of so terrible an evil. Do not live in confu-*

*sion or in fear. Recommend yourselves to the Heart of Jesus, since it is by Him that you will be saved. May His path be your path. Amen!* (8/22/88, #1495).

Briefly, the tempter sets a trap on the road of the salutary covenant, but he will not triumph.

*Every defeat of yours in order to reach Our Lord is a victory of the evil one. The Lord suffers if you allow yourselves to be convinced. Strengthen yourselves, so that you may not succumb to his power; stay away from evil thoughts. Reinforce your faith from day to day for the Lord. Allow the Holy Spirit to work in you. Amen. I say this for the whole world.* (1/9/84, #20).

*You know, my daughter, a tempest, a terrible tempest, work of the devil, has been unleashed. The fact is that the Word of the Lord is an obstacle for many sinners. But I say to you again, what I have told you so many times, the work of the Lord is great and there is no evil capable of stopping it. Amen. Amen!* (4/6/86, #848).

*My poor children, there are few among you who try to go to the heart of Christ, and many among you who are strongly destroyed by sin.*

*Truly, this time is a precious time. It should not be wasted, but one should profit from it, for the Redeemer offers humanity the way of confronting death, which is only Satan, as He did it after the Cross. He also offers it His own mother: Mediatrix of all graces.*

*My dear children, my heart wishes to see your soul live forever and ever.* (1/5/87, #1066).

The last word of Our Lady is the victory of Christ over the powers of darkness:

*The enemy has already been attacked; its end is near. He takes advantage of his last chance by availing himself of human weakness—pride. However, I am going to fight him and I have already begun to fight him. The world must know it. The mother of Christ will triumph over Satan, because near her will be found all the humble sons of her Son.* (2/17/89, #1609).

## Hope

The message of San Nicolás, then, is less a signal of distress than a message of hope and of confidence—the demanding confidence of a struggle. It is the leitmotif of the whole message.

Mary does not stop referring to Christ, Who is "the Morning Star." (12/17/83, #9). She observed:

> *The radiant Star is my Son. Tell it to the whole world: may it not let this Star pass by without following it, for the Lord wants to redeem mankind.* (12/17/83, #9).

This hope is rooted in this place. Gladys informed a priest about the apparition on October 12, 1983, anniversary of the discovery of America, nine years before the celebration of the second millennium. It is within this context that the hope of a new evangalization lies. The star which guided Christopher Columbus is a symbol of a star which is Christ.

Mary invites one to hope:

> *The Lord is revealing through the messages and Holy Scriptures what He expects from mankind. Do not close the doors to Him. Abandon yourselves to Jesus, as He abandoned Himself to you. Make known what I give you. He who wants to believe, let him believe, and he who wants to hear, let him hear. Amen! Read 2 Samuel 23:2-7.* (1/27/84, #32).

She encourages:

> *My daughter, there is a moving answer to the Lord among your people. I see a sincere repentance in many sinners. The goodness of God will manifest itself in those hearts, and the Lord will show that there are no sufferings near Him. I see that my children are sensitive, that they are going to pray with devotion.* (3/16/85, #503).

## *Toward An Era Of Peace*

The message of the covenant announces an era of grace and of peace:

> *Look toward the rising sun and you will see the birth of a new day. Let there be hope and faith in you. And may the desire to be true children of God grow each morning. Do not permit Him to turn away His face from you. Trust in Him. Read Isaiah* 6:9 *and* 65:17-19. (1/25/84, #30).
>
> *My dear children, you are living your earthly life with a great peace in your heart. I assure you that you will not go back, because Christ has entered in you. Children, continue to sow. Glory to God.* (1/26/85, #456).

> *I want to pass through the door which separates me from many of my children, of those who say they are abandoned by the Lord, and of those who, thinking that they are powerful, reject Him.*
>
> *Listen, I come as your help. I am speaking the words of the Lord [. . .].*
>
> *That is why the Lord wants to give peace to the world by giving peace to souls.* (10/25/85, #706).

## *Help Of Christians*

> *My child, as the 'Help of Christians,' I want to redeem my children, asking them for conversion*

*and then consecration to my heart as Mother [. . .]. I will respond to your consecration with my protection.* (8/21/87, #1242).

*A new time has begun. A new hope has been born; attach yourselves to this hope.* (10/14/87, #1277).

*The lost sheep of the Lord are many and He wants to recover them. That is why the Great Shepherd tells those who are in His flock not to leave it, and not to move from His side.* (12/18/83, #10).

For **Mary is the Church**. (3/18/87, #1129). She was its point of departure. She remains the model, the prototype, the sign of its unity.

## *The Church And The Pope*

She depends on the Pope as the guardian of the unity of the Church:

*All of you are a part of the Mystical Body which is the Church, and of which Christ is the Head. On Earth the Vicar of my Son is responsible for that Body to continue; that is why you should follow your Pope closely, following his teaching which is definitely the teaching of Christ. May the Will of my Son be done.* (10/8/87, #1273).

The Blessed Virgin incessantly shows her vigilant love for her dear Church as a continuation of her earthly task near Christ, and for the Pope who has the heavy responsibility for it:

*Pray for the Holy Church. My heart is wounded because it is often attacked. Its light becomes pale from day to day. Since I am Mother of the Church, my sorrow is overwhelming. My sufferings are united to those of the Pope, because his sorrow is my sorrow. The very intense light of Christ is going to be reborn, for just as on Calvary, after crucifixion and death, the Resurrection took place. The Church, too, will be born again through the strength of Love. Amen.* (7/10/88, #1460).

The Blessed Virgin often speaks of the Pope:

*Pray for him, my most predilect son, who has dedicated body and soul to the Lord and to Mary, Mother of Christ. John Paul II, who carries his own cross, takes the peace and the hope of Christ to all peoples, aware of all the dangers to which he is exposed, and humbly continues to consolidate the Church of my Son.* (7/12/86, #917).

On October 27th, the day of the meeting in Assisi, she supported prayer and the Pope's plan:

*My dearest daughter, today prayer will grow in a generous manner. Today, the Pope, knowing what the Lord expects of him, struggles for peace—this most desirable peace which the world needs so much. My beloved children, the priests must follow the Pope, for to walk by him is to walk by my Son Himself.* (10/27/86, #1005).

On the following day, October 28, 1986, Gladys prayed for the Pope. The Blessed Virgin speaks to her about him like a mother:

*My daughter, he is a little child which has entered and continues to grow in the heart of Mary. His fragile body is strengthened with the strength which my love gives. His spirit, completely healthy, intact, and pure, has been given to the Lord. John Paul is a humble servant, his heart overflows with love to and for all. His transparent eyes allow one to see his limpid soul. On his shoulders he carries the great responsibility of the Church and of humanity. He presents it to Christ, and places it in Christ's hands. The world is in need of peace. The world needs love. Christ gives peace; Christ offers His love.* (10/28/86, #1006).

Regarding the visit of the Pope to Argentina (April 16, 1987), Our Lady honored the Holy Father with these words:

*My child, this day will be marked in the history of your country, and in the heart of all Christians. The Vicar of Christ arrives with humility, with his heart filled with kindness. His mouth speaks of Christ; his heart loves what Christ loves and his feet walk the steps of Christ. The Mother is near her predilect Son. Glory to God.* (4/6/87, #1145; likewise numbers 1149, 1273, 1334, 1403, 1460, 1635, 1678).

*THE MESSAGE—PART 4*

# The Means And The Weapons

## *. . .Through Prayer*

The Blessed Virgin invited us to prayer insistently.

> *Pray only. I place before your eyes the manner of bearing suffering and of alleviating it.* (9/16/86, #969).
>
> *One cannot live without offering a daily prayer to Our Father in Heaven, or also with hatreds and rancor. Hasten to the Lord in everything that you need. He listens to all those who pray with faith. Read James* 1:2-12. (12/21/83, #13).

Our Lady has always recommended prayer as the chief weapon to defeat Satan. San Nicolás is no different. She continues her appeals:

> *If your prayer is said with Christian love, it will be efficacious. Pray in company with my maternal Heart.* (3/20/89, #1628).
>
> *My daughter, the suffering of the poor strikes my heart—the sadness of the disinherited, of the marginal. All cause anguish to my heart of a mother [. . .]. You will find in prayer the strength for your spirit. In prayer you will discover the Mother who awaits her children. Pray and you will remain close to God.* (6/6/89, #1668).

*My children, I ask you for prayers for a soul who is not praying and decreases in love of God. Let no one pretend to be agreeable to God if he is far from God. I ask for prayers and the conversion of hearts.* (9/23/89, #1714).

*Gladys, pray for my errant children. Pray so that each heart will permit the love of my Son to enter, so that rebellion may cease.* (10/3/89, #1725).

## ***. . .Through the Rosary***

Our Lady particularly recommends the prayer of the Holy Rosary:

*Recite the Holy Rosary, and let the Lord see that with it goes your conversion. The Sacred Heart of Jesus will give you abundant blessings.* (1/18/84, #25).

It is a victorious weapon and a way toward love. On April 10, 1986, Gladys wrote:

"I see an enormous crown of white rosaries. I see the Most Blessed Virgin and she tells me:" *You see this crown because this is what I want you to do, a real crown of rosaries. Pray, my daughter, pray. How many mouths remain silent, still without even knowing a single prayer which may bring them close to the Lord! The Holy Rosary is the weapon which the enemy fears. It is also the refuge of those who look for relief for their sufferings, and it is the door to enter into my heart. Glory to the Lord for the Light which He gives the world.* (4/10/86, #850).

On June 6, 1987, the day when the Pope recited the Rosary, transmitted on Mondivision, she stated:

*My daughter, in these moments, there is an extreme need of prayer. The Holy Rosary will be heard this day by the Lord as though it were my voice. Prayer is a request of mine and it is directed to all peoples. Prayer must be born from a willing heart. It must also be frequent and made with love. Never put it aside, since the mother wants her children to go to God by means of it, and it is the weapon which she uses and with which she succeeds in conquering the enemy.* (#1192).

The Blessed Virgin insists:

*You cannot imagine what the value of prayer is [. . .]. Recite the Holy Rosary while meditating on its Mysteries, and I assure you that your prayers will be elevated, like a true hymn of love, to the Lord. Glory to the Lord.* (6/13/85, #585).

On the day after, she suggested that "a perpetual rosary be recited during the 24 hours of the twenty-fifth of each month [. . .] without interruption." (6/14/85, #586).

*It is a refuge in suffering.* (4/10/86, #850).
*It is a "contemplative prayer."* (12/1/87 and 12/2/87, #1309-1310).
*It is the beginning of growth.* (9/3/89, #1701).

She comments thus on the Joyful Mysteries:

**The Annunciation:** *Never as on that day when the Angel Gabriel told me that I would be the Mother of God, through the power of the Holy Spirit, have I experienced similar joy. I did not understand, and still my faith, my great faith, permitted me to immediately say* **Yes.**

**My visitation to Elizabeth** [. . .]: *She called me 'blessed among women,' and it is thus that they still call me, and that they will call me always, throughout Eternity.*

**The Birth of Jesus:** *After having spent long hours looking for shelter, we arrived with Joseph at this stable and there, during this very cold night, Jesus was born, very poorly, being kept warm by my warmth as a mother.*

**Jesus is Presented in the Temple:** *Joseph, my Child, and I went there. Simeon was there. He prophesied to me that the sword would pierce my heart.* (*Lk.* 2:35).

**After having thought that He was lost:** *We find Jesus again. We found Him again, preaching the Word of His Father among the Doctors of the Law. At the age of 12 He was already the best and the most faithful of the preachers. My Son filled me with joy from the moment of His Annunciation, and He still fills me with joy by permitting me to be near Him today, in order to call souls to conversion.* (1/25/88, #1342).

Mary often returned to these mysteries and to Jesus' youth. On October 4, 1986 (#983), she recalls that Christmas night:

*My daughter, you do not know how many sufferings we endured with my spouse Joseph! We did not have friends, or shelters for lodging. Only bad weather accompanied us, and then that stable which was converted into a cradle for my Son and an asylum for us. That night, which was sad and silent, was for Joseph and for me, the most beautiful. It would also be for the world, since there the Savior of mankind was born. The Just among the just and the Lord over everything.* (10/4/86, #983).

On May 2, 1985, it was the growth of the Child Jesus:

"The Blessed Virgin tells me how Jesus was when He was a Child [. . .]:"

*At three years of age He was endowed with a great intelligence; He had the understanding which God the Father gave Him. He grew up knowing that He was the Son of God. He was always very quiet, always meditating, but when He spoke He did it with humility and a great wisdom, the great*

*Wisdom of God. My daughter, that is the way that my beloved Son was on Earth.* (5/2/85, #546).

On August 5, 1988, she recalled her maternal concerns and the departure of Jesus for His public life:

*The more time passes, the more my presence is necessary for mankind. This mother* (Mary speaks of herself in the third person) *worries very much for her children, just as I worried very much for Jesus when He was little.*

*I had an extreme care for Him. I did not leave Him; He did not leave me. Joseph and I loved Him with a very tender love. Later, when He had grown, very much time had passed before He returned close to me. He had the stars for a roof. His knees served Him as a pillow. He was not afraid of persecutions. Nothing worried Him, except if it were not to transmit the promise of the Father. This same Jesus travelled over roads trying to reach hearts, to convert souls.*

*Today it is the Mother of Heaven who comes down to convert souls. Today it is her heart of a Mother who protects her children, and the heart of a mother loves and wants to be loved with the heart of the Son. Blessed be the Savior!* (#1480).

And on May 12, 1987:

*When He was on Earth, my Son lived only for the things of Heaven. Nothing material attached Him to the things of the Earth. He knew indeed that He had to live His time with men, and they were His last years, those which He dedicated completely to be a Shepherd, to unite the flock of God, His Father. [. . .]. All those who have not yet understood the importance which the flock of the Lord has, may they understand the value of the union of that flock so loved by my Son.* (#1171).

On January 18, 1989, it is the voice of Jesus which commented on the Sorrowful Mysteries:

**First Mystery:** *I prayed only that the Will of My Father be fulfilled.*

**Second Mystery:** *In spite of the offenses, I accepted everything out of love.*

**Third Mystery:** *While the outrages and the mockery followed, I suffered out of love.*

**Fourth Mystery:** *I was stoned and, at each fall, I prayed to My Father so that He might forgive those who insulted Me.*

**Fifth Mystery:** *My love grew while My strength was giving out. I experienced the cold of death in My Body and, at the same time, the Will of My Father was being fulfilled. My Body was going to be glorified. It went away to Him.*

*At the present time, I am in each tabernacle. My Body wishes to be adored there, just as in each Eucharistic Sacrifice. It wants to be the eternal food for souls until I definitely go to them.* (1/17/89, #1599).

On August 3, 1988, it was Our Lady who commented on the Glorious Mysteries.

*You see, Gladys, on the day of the Crucifixion of my Son, my suffering was great.*

*But the emotion of* **His Resurrection** *was even greater. He had already announced it to His disciples. I was expecting it, knowing that He would rise. I never doubted His Word. After the great suffering, it was joy in the certainty that He would be in the heights near His Father.*

**The Ascension of Jesus:** *He is in Heaven Body and Soul, and from there, He observes the hearts and penetrates them in order to be able to act according to His designs.*

**The Descent of the Holy Spirit:** *The Holy Spirit descended while I was praying with the apostles, and the Holy Spirit strengthened their spirits.*

**I was taken up to Heaven,** *body and soul also, thanks to the mercy of the Father, to the love of the Son, and to the power of the Holy Spirit. After Heaven, in my glorified body near my Son, I intercede for the needs of children.*

**I am the Mother of everything that has been created by God.** *I am the Woman clothed in the sun, the new Eve, she who will lead mankind to the Light. She who will make Eternity accessible to them. Amen. Amen! Make it known.* (#1479).

### *. . .Through Conversion*

Prayer is inseparable from conversion. It is the basic act through which we turn away from sin in order to turn to God. And conversion is always stressed by Our Lady. It is her mission:

> *You have been called in order to be bearers of peace and in order that the urgent call from Christ Jesus for the conversion of man be known. I am concerned for the whole world. Remember that only the Lord will save you. Read Jonah* 4:11 *and Micah* 6:8-9 (12/30/83, #15).

Our Lady insists:

> *I want the conversion of the world. No longer disobey the Lord. My dear children, pray so that it may be so.* (2/24/88, #63).

On March 21, 1988, Gladys received a broad vision on the conversion of the world:

> "I see the Earth cut into two parts: one part represents the two thirds, and the other one third. On it I see the Most Blessed Virgin with the Child. From her breast some luminous rays come

toward the part which represents the two thirds of the Earth. Immediately she tells me:" *Gladys, you are in the process of seeing the world half destroyed. My heart emits its rays of light in order to save the most souls possible. My heart is all powerful; but it cannot do anything if the soul refuses it. There are two ways to save the soul: prayer and conversion.* (3/21/88, #1377).

## . . .Through Penance

Conversion is inseparable from penance, and there you have two aspects of the same act. Penance includes:

— The negative: regret, detachment, asceticism, a pulling away from the slavery of sin;
— The positive: conversion which turns the heart of sinners to God:

*Know how to carry your cross. Accept it as He accepted it. Read Peter* 4:1-2 *and* 7 *until the end.* (11/28/83, #2).

On October 13, 1984, she invited us to reconciliation, forgiveness, conversion, the sacrament of penance:

*These days are favorable days in order to open your hearts to the Lord. Take advantage of them in order to go to confession, and to repent for every evil action, and be able to find a new life in Christ.* (10/13/84, #325).

*It is love which makes penance light. The greater the love that there is in you, the lighter will be what you will have to endure. Near God, suffering, bitterness, and even defeat do not exist.* (4/11/85, #526).

This call to penance is then a stranger to all moroseness. It is the sportlike impulse of which St. Paul speaks (*1 Cor.* 9:24-27). It is willingly that the runner hastens toward his goal, however severe his effort may be:

*You must know how to hope in the Lord. He tests His children, but He does not leave them without help. The sweetness of His love is shed over you. My children, may bitterness not be your companion; may your sorrow not be reflected in tears. Celebrate the approaching which the Lord permits you toward Him.* (7/6/85, #608).

But difficulties themselves cooperate for the good of those who accept them in Jesus Christ.

*God sends trials because trials strengthen weaknesses. God speaks of love and hope, because the love of the Father is united to the hope of salvation which His Son offers.* (Words of Jesus, 9/23/85, #677).

As Christmas 1987 approached, Our Lady again encouraged contrition of heart and confession:

*Today, My Son wants to be welcomed, as He was that night in Bethlehem, with humility, but also with all the love with which men are capable. During the novena* [from December 16-25], *prepare your hearts through prayer, confession, and Holy Communion, in order to worthily receive the Son of God.* (12/9/87, #1318).

On the Feast of Our Lady of Sorrows, September 15, 1989:

*My daughter, in these days, here are my sorrows: the refusal of my Son, atheism, the lack of charity, the children which one prevents from being born, the lack of understanding in families, the great egotism of many of my children in the world, the hearts which are closed to the love of their Mother. Children, console my sorrow as a mother. Blessed be the Most High.* (9/15/89, #1707).

At this time, when the Father of the prodigal children is multiplying His mercies, the Blessed Virgin invites one to do the same:

*I say to all your brothers:*

— *In imitation of the saints, practice mercy. The humble man glorifies himself in God and not in his own works.*

— *If the spirit resupplies itself in God, it will function in accordance with the Will of God.* (11/1/89, #1741).

## . . .Through the Word

The Blessed Virgin teaches, that it is the Word of Christ which nourishes and guides faith and conversion.

*If I point out to you biblical readings at the same time as my messages, it is so that the world may understand that they are authentic, and that it may not cause doubt in you. My Son Jesus looks for their conversion.*

*Study these readings again in order to find in them answers which, for the time being, escape you* (on that day she has her read *Haggai* 1:5-7 and 2:23). (1/14/84, #22).

*Atheism is inundating nations. Everywhere, God is absent. That is why the Word of God must be listened to and not despised. The action of His Word can be very powerful if hearts open up.* (2/27/88, #1363).

## . . .Through the Eucharist

This profound unity, to which the Blessed Virgin invites us, is accomplished through the Eucharist where Christ, Eternal Word of God, gives Himself completely.

On November 11, 1985 (#721), then on the 17th (#726), the message insists on the importance of Communion:

*It is for your love, strength, and life. You have just been nourished by the most Precious Food.* (#726).

On November 27, 1985, during the second elevation of the Mass, Our Lady exhorted Gladys:

*It is with the blessing of God the Father that today you will be nourished by my Son.* (#736).

On January 29, 1986, she proclaimed:

*Jesus Who is exposed is accessible to all!* (#791).

During the Mass of March 9, 1986, when the priest raised the ciborium for Communion, Jesus told Gladys:

*Behold My Body which is going to meet my brothers.* (#820).

On June 1, 1986, Mary stated specifically:

*Jesus, the Eucharist! It is His living and true Body; adore It and love It. My dear children, it is in the Eucharist that you will be able to experience how much He gives Himself to you. It is in the Eucharist that He becomes again Body and Blood, and it is through the Eucharist that He wants to save the souls which are ready to receive Him.* (#888).

On August 2, 1988 (#1478), she thus exalts this gift:

*Oh, my dear child, how Jesus loves souls! He loves them so much, that no love exceeds the love of the Lord.*

*Love which gives Himself, Love divine, burning Love.*

*Love which every soul can receive in the Holy Eucharist.*

*Love which He offers in the Holy Sacrifice of the Eucharist.*

*Love which wants to be union.*

*Love which exceeds every human understanding.*

On September 12, 1988, she invited us to adoration:

> *Adore the Body and Blood of my Son in the Most Blessed Sacrament: a marvelous mystery which all do not understand, a marvelous mystery of Love, offered each day in the Holy Eucharist. It is the moment when suffering and joy come together [. . .]: suffering opposite the knowledge of His death, joy from the conquering knowledge of death.*
>
> *The soul must approach Christ. The soul must unite itself to Christ each day, and for that, there is nothing better than Holy Communion: the Food of the soul for life.* (#1511).

On May 28, 1989, on the Feast of Corpus Christi, she asked:

> *Let all of humanity go to meet the Love of God. Let there be no indifference in your hearts, but love. I say to all your brothers: come, I am going to show you the great Love. I am going to teach you how to adore Jesus, how to receive Him in the Holy Eucharist, so necessary for the soul.* (#1663).

On August 19, 1989, she invited "all her children" to "be nourished with the Bread of Life": the Holy Eucharist. (#1797).

On February 2, 1990, nine days before the end of the messages, she invited us to daily Communion. (#1797).

## . . .Through Fraternal Love

Christ and His Eucharist lead to unity through fraternal love. But today our love of one another is often in decay. On January 31, 1984, Gladys had this vision:

> "I see a large hall with many people—young men and women who appear to be drunk. It is frightful. The Blessed Virgin tells me:"

*These are calamities, human prey. No son from fit parents should come to these places. God is not here, or in places such as this. No one is looking for the Lord in this place. You must pray for the young people of the world who have not found God, for those who behave in a disparaging way, for those who are badly advised. The Lord can rescue them because He is merciful and loves His children. Read Galatians* 6:2-10. (#38).

And still:

*He who curses, who hates, is only poisoning his heart. Let no one curse, hate; let there be no evil thought in your thoughts. Forgive as Jesus forgives; love as the Lord loves you. Look for perfection in Him.* (4/3/85, #520).

In San Nicolás, Our Lady is basically only repeating and bringing into reality her words to the servants at Cana: *"Do everything that He will tell you."* (*Jn.* 2:5).

## *In the Wake of Fatima*

Mary's prophetic message follows in the wake of the apparitions of Fatima, which occurred during the First World War (May 13-October 13, 1917). In San Nicolás, Mary spoke for the first time on October 13, 1983, anniversary of the last apparition of Fatima. This synchronism stresses the historical and prophetic significance of the apparition. The Blessed Virgin today follows the objective which she had already formulated in Portugal: *"My heart will triumph."*

On May 13, 1989, anniversary of the first apparition at Fatima, she explicitly stated at San Nicolás:

*My daughter, as previously in Fatima, today my visits are renewed on Earth. They are more frequent and more prolonged, because humanity is passing through very dramatic times.*

*Has man not understood that he must be uniquely at the service of God? If he resists, his soul is going to perish.*

*Many hearts do not accept my invitation to prayer and to conversion. That is why the work of the devil is growing and is expanding. My dear children, it is only through prayer and conversion that you will return to God. May He not find your hearts dry.* (5/13/89, #1655).

## . . .Through Consecration

Our Lady invites us to a true consecration. It is the root of all holiness. Consecration is our deification for Eternity. God alone, then, is its beginning and end.

On February 12, 1988, she states **her** specific role in this consecration:

*My daughter, when a heart opens up to the heart of a mother, it stays there. When a heart abandons itself to the heart of a mother, she will shape it and guide it to her Son. In this heart will be found purity, love, humility, for it deals with the heart of her who loves her Son, and who obeys Him.* (#1353).

If at times the Blessed Virgin refers consecration to her Immaculate Heart, it is as a relay, a way, a path to God, for eventually it is a consecration (deification) only to God, and through God. And the message of Mary expresses this fundamental truth very well; whence this prayer which she inspires in Gladys on August 10, 1986:

"Most beloved Mother, teach me to love Jesus. Make me worthy of Jesus and of you, my Mother! And may the consecration of this day unite me more to you and your Son. Amen!"

To Christ, first of all, and in Him, to Mary.

"Afterwards, she said to me:"

*Your brothers can recite this prayer on the day of their consecration to my Heart. The consecration will not deprive the Christian of his freedom. It will not annihilate it. But it will make him grow interiorly. It will permit spiritual renewal of each day. It will allow it to introduce itself into my heart, and to nourish itself there completely. Thus they will love Jesus in a total manner by passing through my heart. My heart gives and it demands, but it does not ask for the impossible.* (8/10/86, #939).

Mary is at the service of the supreme and gratuitous freedom of God, and of the freedom of mankind, which cannot be fulfilled except in harmony with the Supreme Freedom. Our deification is inscribed in the wake of the basic consecration—that which Jesus made of His humanity, and of all humanity in the womb of Mary, on the day of the Annunciation through the hypostatic union.

God, Who alone consecrates, does not do anything without us. Consecration is then also a free act, our irreplaceable commitment. It is done through prayer.

*This is what I tell those who are consecrated to me:*

*Renew yourself through prayer, through an intense prayer.*

*I want perseverance, I want fidelity, I want authentic consecrated souls. I want you with me; you have approached my heart. You have introduced yourselves into my heart; continue in it. Offer, my children, together with your love, your spirit of penance.* (3/24/87, #1135).

The request becomes more pressing beginning in 1988:

*This consecration does not demand either paper or formula, because this consecration will go straight to my heart [. . .]. It will only be received by my heart.* (5/25/88, day of the monthly pilgrimage, #1426).

On October 13, 1988, fifth anniversary of her first words, Our Lady insisted:

> *Gladys, I am the mother, who since she spoke to you the first day and since then, does not cease to speak words of faith in God, at the same time calling men to prayer and to conversion.*
>
> *Mankind must understand that these messages reinforce the love of the Mother of Heaven for her children. These messages must be received in humility with an open heart.*
>
> *It is good that my children know that I ask them for consecration since, when they are consecrated to my heart, they belong also to the mother as well as to the Son. My own light will remove all darkness by permitting my children to walk on the path which God has established.* (10/13/88, #1534).

Consecration to the Heart of Mary is understood in this sense, that the Heart of the Word Incarnate, corporally formed in Mary, and the heart of Mary, spiritually formed through Christ, are *only one Heart.* That is why St. John Eudes speaks of it in the singular: *"the Heart of Jesus and Mary."*

One of the last messages (February 2, 1990) exhorts those who are committed through vows in consecration:

> *I ask my consecrated children to give their mother everything that she requests.*
>
> *That they devote at least an hour each day to prayer.*
>
> *That they receive Communion daily.*
>
> *That they be humble.*
>
> *That they be at the complete service of Mary.*
>
> *That they be pleasing to God each day by living as consecrated souls.*
>
> *That they be united to the Love of her Son.*

*That they ask for the Grace to live under the Light of the Holy Spirit.*

*The consecration must be made on a special feast of the Mother. Such is the consecration which I ask in my sanctuary.* (#1798).

*THE MESSAGE—PART 5*

# With Christ To The Father

## *An Exchange with Christ*

The message of San Nicolás is an exchange between the 1,804 messages of the Blessed Virgin and the 68 messages of Christ (generally shorter, stronger, more essential). They are a strong echo of the message of the Gospel. Jesus repeats it and Mary leads to it, pedagogically, tirelessly through her word, indefatigable, like that of a mother.

Where Christ speaks, she comments humbly. She is completely at His service. She guides to Him and through Him to the Father under the influence of the Holy Spirit, Who radically invested her from her Immaculate Conception, to the Annunciation (*Lk.* 1:35), then to Pentecost (*Acts* 1:14 and 2:1-12).

## *The Return of Christ*

The messages invite us to wait for the return of Christ—*"the coming of the Lord is imminent,"* and although we know *"neither the day nor the hour"* (*Matt.* 24:36), it is necessary *"to prepare oneself for it."* And such would be the very reason for the apparitions as Our Lady specifically states here. (3/26/88, #1382 already cited on p. 57).

> *Jesus came to the world out of love, and His second coming for His greater glory will take place likewise because of love. Open your hearts and let Him enter. Alleluia!* (12/25/88, #1584).

*Keep Jesus company by drinking His Chalice. Open the doors of your heart. Prepare your spirit so as to be able to receive the glorious coming of my Son some day.* (4/28/89, #1648).

## Through the Holy Spirit

The Holy Spirit, intimate Mover in the work of Salvation, and very close to the Blessed Virgin, appears from the very first messages: November 1, 1983. (Pérez #4).

Then the Blessed Virgin (temple icon and harp of the Holy Spirit) insistently refers to it.

*Today the Holy Spirit will nourish you.* (11/17/83, Pérez #9). *The Holy Spirit is your Guide; you must obey Him.* (11/25/83, Pérez #17).

On November 29, 1983, the Blessed Virgin invited Gladys to read *Acts* 1:8:

*You will receive the strength of the Holy Spirit Who will descend. You will be my witnesses [. . .] until the ends of the earth.* (Pérez #22).

And she continued to persist:

*Invoke the Holy Spirit and He will save you.* (12/12/83, #4). *Allow the Holy Spirit to work in you.* (1/9/84, #20).

All along He retains a significant place, for it is in Him and through Him that Christ was made flesh in Mary (*Lk.* 1:35), that Christ began His ministry, and it is in Him that Christ continues to work for the salvation of mankind:

*Glorify the Holy Spirit with a heart full of joy, for He is living today and always. The Holy Spirit has come to clean with the fire of His Love, the souls whom the evil one tries to drag away from their own purification. Nothing is going to stand as an obstacle to His almighty strength to work in them. Every gift comes from the Spirit; it is in the Spirit that one comes to love.* (6/7/87, #1193. See also 3/28/89, #1637).

## *The Trinity*

The message of San Nicolás completely refers us to the Trinity. Since 1983, the Blessed Virgin invited Gladys to say this prayer:

*Blessed be the Father and the Son and the Holy Spirit. It is in the midst of the Holy Trinity that you will find Peace and eternal life.* (12/6/83, Pérez #30).

During a fasting of three days, which makes her thoroughly receptive to the Holy Spirit, Our Lady tells her:

*It is not a penance. It is the spiritual preparation which the Lord asks of you.* (ibid).

The messages regarding the Trinity continue:

*I ask my children to love and to glorify the Most Holy Trinity. Do not look for an answer to that which is forbidden to mankind. The Most Holy Trinity remains the Secret of God. Only He knows it and it only belongs to Him alone. Glory to the Father, to the Son, and to the Holy Spirit.* (6/13/87, #1198).

*I ask my children to believe in the Holy Trinity, to love the Most Holy Trinity. Love the Father, Creator of Heaven and Earth; love the Son, Redeemer of mankind; love the Holy Spirit, Light of Hope. The child cannot be strengthened if it is not through the Father. He can save his soul only if the Son saves it. He can renew his spirit only if the Spirit Himself renews him. Glorify the Triune God. May He be praised and blessed forever and ever.* (7/11/88, #1461).

According to this recommendation, Gladys received the inspiration for a prayer, on December 6, 1988, the Feast of St. Nicholas:

> *Glory to the Father:*
> *Father, I glorify You for everything that You have created.*
> *Glory to the Son Jesus Christ:*
> *To You be glory for Your sorrowful Passion, for abandonment to the Father, and for Your Ressurection.*
> *Glory to the Holy Spirit:*
> *Glory to You for the Light which You give to the world, for the love which You spread in the world.*
> *Blessed be You, one and triune God, because of Your great mercy.* (12/6/88, #1568)..

On the same day, December 6th, the Blessed Virgin told Gladys:

> *My heart of a mother claims the love of my children, toward the Most Blessed Trinity:*
> *God the Father: Power and Love,*
> *God the Son: Love thirsting for love,*
> *Holy Spirit: Light and Love.*
> *The Holy Trinity perfectly shows the love of God for souls. Most Holy Trinity, so often rejected and denied! Walk under Its splendor which reflects so much love.* (12/6/88, #1569).

On the Feast of the Holy Trinity, Mary, Its holy temple par excellence, invited her to meet this supreme love:

> *I let all your brothers know that the Holy Trinity wants to come to all of the souls through the intermediary of my heart. The perfect love of the Father, of the Son, and of the Holy Spirit wants to purify us. Respond to this proof of love, invisible but real;* [let this be your response], *visible and sincere—your conversion.* (5/21/89, #1658).

*THE MESSAGE—PART 6*

# Salvation Through The Cross In Faith

## *Universal Salvation*

St. Paul says that God wants all to be saved (*1 Tim.* 2:4). The perspective of universal salvation, given by God, dominates the messages from the beginning. It is a recurring theme:

> *The Lord gives His light. Permit it to illuminate you and it will deliver the sinner from all chastisement. In His time the Lord will make known the greatness of His works.* (2/19/84, #56).
>
> *You ask yourselves whether the Lord can forgive those who forget His existence. And I say to you: yes, my dear children, the Lord can do it because of His great mercy. Yet, do not abuse the goodness of God, and cling to my mantle with strength for it will really cleanse you, and will present you pure before the Lord.* (2/28/86, #811).

And still on September 16, 1986:

> *God all powerful will save him who recognizes the Lord, as well as the unbeliever. Blessed be His power!* (#969).

She invites us to rely on her, her loving presence as mother in the sanctuary of San Nicolás:

*My daughter, it is because of a minority of good people that many evil ones will find salvation. Through prayer, I mean to say, through the persevering prayer of true Christians, many will be saved. Such is the reason for my presence and the meaning of my messages which are eventually the Word of the Lord.* (12/15/86, #1046).

## The Cross

The work of Salvation comes through the Cross. Our Lady was, and remains, completely involved with it.

On November 25, 1983, she said to Gladys:

*I have suffered very much as Mother, but the Almighty has rewarded me with Eternity.* (Pérez #16).

Her suffering was the compassion and the transfixion of Calvary. It is also the sins of the children which Jesus gave to her in exchange from the Cross at the moment before He left through His death. That is why she invites us to live this Mystery:

*My dear children, during this novena* (from March 17-25), *I ask you to keep Jesus company on the Cross, and to keep me company as the Sorrowful Mother. Jesus. the Holy One of my heart, had planned that I be the mother of all mankind while I was at the foot of the Cross. Since then, from your cradle, I try to lead you; I go in search of those who do not want to find me. During this novena* [which ends on Holy Tuesday, during Passion week], *you will only meditate on the Sorrowful Mysteries. Blessed be the Lamb of God.* (3/10/86, #821).

And on the same day (#822):

*The suffering of the Crucifixion of Jesus increases in me. You cannot imagine how much they mistreated Him, like the most cruel of evildoers, the worst of sinners. He, Son of the Eternal Father, without the least stain of sin! My daughter, what painful cry of suffering was mine when a lance pierced His Heart. Facing the crowd which surrounded Him, He found Himself without the least defense. What love then, that of God for men, what love then, that of Jesus for His brothers! He knew that it was necessary for Him to subject Himself because of them, in order to be able to redeem them and to lead them near His Father forever, for eternity.*

*On the Cross, death transformed itself into life. Glory to God forever and ever!* (3/10/86, #822).

The Cross then, has its place in the life of those who are to find the way of Salvation:

*I look at my children who claim the graces from the Lord, and I say to them: just pray. I am going to put before your eyes the manner of enduring the suffering, and of alleviating it.* (9/16/86, #969).

## Faith

The Blessed Virgin recalls trials and suffering only in order to restore faith. She does not waste time on prescriptions. Thus she speaks of fasting only once, on January 11, 1989 (#1594, as we have seen). It is trust in God, in His love, in the maternal love of Mary, which dominates and runs through all her messages from the beginning.

*Bless the Lord, King of the Universe. Praise God Our Father. All of you know that He is merciful. In Him is pardon, and He loves you above all things. Know that His kingdom is eternal; just as His love which He proves for His children is eternal. He claims only your faith, and He wants to see you live according to His Word. In exchange, He recommends to you salvation of the soul, and complete liberation. Amen. Amen!* (2/11/84, #48).

*My daughter, how generous the Lord is! His generosity is evident when we consider everything which He gives. The love of God elevates the heart of man. The mercy of God is already manifested among Christians. The life of God is the only life, and it will be so eternally. Preach about it. Amen! Read 2 Corinthians 6:13.* (3/18/87, #1129).

## Health of Body and Soul

The Blessed Virgin does not cease to speak as "mother." She often gives herself this title when speaking of herself in the third person: "The Mother loves you," "the Mother asks you." This good mother has formed, nourished, raised the Body of Christ. She comes to alleviate our bodies in the wake of Christ, so concerned about illnesses in the Gospel. She is there in the traditional prayers of votive Masses of the Blessed Virgin, when one asks Mary for her intercession for "the health of body and soul":

*My dear children, the day will come when you will be called by the Lord. Your mother desires that on that day, He will find your body and your soul in good health. Offer yourselves to the Lord and, little by little, He is going to change your hearts. Pray:*

*With Christ on my side,*
*My weakness disappears.*
*His Love nourishes me*
*And multiplies my strength.*
*I give thanks to Jesus*
*Who has known how to awaken me.* (8/27/84, #262).

Likewise, on September 29, 1989, Feast of the Archangels, the Blessed Virgin observed their role in this manner:

*They defend the soul from the perils of the devil; they open in the soul a way of light in the midst*

> *of darkness. They restore health of body and prepare the soul to desire spiritual salvation with the greatest intensity.* (#1720).

These messages do not separate the health of the soul from that of the body. They associate both with the conversion of the heart which is its instrument. From there we have so many cures in the wake of the Gospel.

Mary carries all of these intentions in her heart as mother. She has chosen San Nicolás in order to fulfill them. It is a place of Mercy.[2]

---

2. SAN NICOLÁS, PLACE OF MERCY, CHOSEN BY MARY. It is the framework of the message, especially numbers 55, 84, 85, 88, 84, 118. *"I have chosen this city as final residence"*; 258, 327, 463, 485, 531, 553, 604, 633, 655, 682, 700, 785, 788, 808, 826, 1029, 1061, 1133, 1183, 1283, 1362, 1383, 1541, 1564, 1594, and August 25, 1989, #1697.

*THE MESSAGE—PART 7*

# Spread And Live The Message

## *Spread the Message*

Our Lady invites us to a worldwide dissemination of her message.

> *Make known what I give you. Let him who wants to believe, believe, and him who wants to understand, understand.* (1/27/84, #32).

> *Some believe that they do not need to read the Word of the Lord and His messages. This hardness of heart is not healthy for you.* (10/11/84, #322).

> *I am your eyes; permit me to show you your way. I am your ears and I will help you to listen to God. In your turn, be my mouth, and preach my messages.* (7/23/85, #621).

On August 31, 1985, it is Jesus Who said:

> *The believers, faithful to the Creator, will find in this message the blessing of God.* (8/31/85, #654).

## *Live the Message*

This same day, the Blessed Virgin added:

> *Do not look for rest day and night. It is necessary to preach.* (ibid).

She insists without respite:

*My daughter, it is necessary to read my messages without hurrying, so that they can be assimilated as I wish.* (1/24/86, #786).

*From here the faith through Jesus and Mary will be reborn. It is from here that I invite the world to look for the Living Fountain, the Fountain of Peace, the Fountain of Grace. I want to cure my children from this illness which is materialism: an illness which makes many suffer. I want to help them to discover Christ, and I want to make it known to them that Christ prevails over everything.* (1/26/86, #788).

*Thanks to God, my words go throughout the world. Thanks to God, you can receive my blessings.* (10/12/86, #990).

*At this time when the poison of the evil one seems to contaminate everything, the Lord manifests Himself so that the salvation of souls may be possible. His Words risk being ineffectual, weakening, if one relegates them, if they are not disseminated. They must be proclaimed all over the earth.* (12/26/88, #1585).

*Gladys, mankind is in the process of falling into a progressive self-destruction. That is why it is necessary, now, to disseminate the words of the Mother. The Lord has marked this time with a sign: the Woman clothed with the sun (Apoc.* 12:1). *She represents the hope to which her children must cling. The Mother has looked on you. It is up to you to set your eyes and your heart on God.* (2/28/89, #1616).

## *Demands of the Kingdom of God*

Mary insists that we make the demands of the Kingdom of God, a central theme in our lives. She states:

> *Here is my kingdom with you. Read attentively my messages [. . .]. I will remain among you, availing myself of you. You will be the bridge of unity. Preach my word. Many will be the blind who do not want to see. Many will be the deaf who do not want to hear. But do not be afraid. Yours is the Kingdom of Heaven.* (11/18/83, first series, #10).

> *My messages will spread the light. It will take some effort from you to learn them. It is a joy to know that they are with the Word of the Lord. Remember, that everything that I ask you will require sacrifices, particularly on your part. I will protect you. The whole Kingdom will protect you [. . .]. I want to be here. It is my place.* (11/24/83, Pérez #16).

On the Feast of the Immaculate Conception, 1983, she encourages:

> *Today must be a day consecrated to prayer. Do not let it go by without accomplishing it. Some difficult days await you, but with the help of the Lord, you will conquer. Walk with your head up high because you walk with the Truth which only the Lord gives. The whole army of the Kingdom accompanies you on this day. Amen. Read Colossians* 1:10 *and* 3:16-17. (12/8/83, Pérez #32).

The Kingdom of God is a seed of grace planted in the inside of man. It becomes tangible by concrete signs of conversion and the fruits that are manifested through these actions.

*CHAPTER 11*

# The End Of The Messages

*(February 11, 1990)*

The some 1800 messages which had begun on October 13, 1983, ended seven years later on February 11, 1990. The last messages were characterized by a certain brevity, and especially by a return to the essential: grace, humility, love, consecration, joy.

## *Humility*

On January 25, 1990, the Blessed Virgin delivered a message which was a beautiful echo of her **Magnificat:** *"He has put down the mighty from their thrones and exalted the humble."* It is a message which grace fulfilled in her, well before she prophesied:

> *Gladys, I talk to my children to ask them for humility.*
> *I ask you for humility, because in humility you will be pleasant in the eyes of God. I ask you for humility because the Lord loves the humble and rejects the proud. Do not resist when it is a matter of being humble. Follow the example of Christ Jesus. Glory be to Him! Read Proverbs 3:34:*
> *He mocks those who mock, but to the humble he gives grace.* (#1794).

## *Faith and Thanksgiving*

On the following day, January 26, 1990, the Virgin Mary repeated her blessings:

> *Blessed are the children who believe in the multitude of divine goods. Blessed are those who listen to the Lord, their help. Blessed are those who glorify His Name; bless each child who believes in God and His mother. Amen. Amen!* (#1795).

## *Consecration Through Love*

Six days later, on February 1, 1990, it is a warning:

> *Gladys, those who do not obey the Mother will suffer pains of death. On the contrary, those who obey her will enjoy the well being of life.*
>
> *For a child of God, there is only the possibility to love, because God Himself calls his love.*
>
> *I tell my children: let me build in your hearts. Glory to the Most High.* (#1796).

The message of the day after, February 2nd (feast day of the Presentation), insists on grace, the principle and moving force of everything else:

> *This is what I say to my children:*
>
> *The grace of God is with you. The grace of His Son, Light of the world, is manifested in His mother.*
>
> *Look at the world today! Many are without my Son; they do not rest in His love. My voice of a mother, deeply anxious for you, invites you to follow Christ. Do not doubt. Go to the Light. Amen. Amen!* (#1797).

This message concludes with a final call to consecration (cited above, pages 95-97).

## ***Love, Prayer, and Joy***

On the following day, February 3rd, the Blessed Virgin insists on prayer and love, theme of all her messages:

> *I tell all your brothers: be fervent and constant in prayer. Offer it to the Lord with love, with your heart, with your suffering. Recall, from my heart there comes forth much love and much prayer to the Father Who is in Heaven. Glory to the Most High. Read 1 Peter 3:12:*
>
> *For the Lord has His eyes on the just, and extends His ear to their prayer; but the face of the Lord is against the evil doers.* (#1799).

On February 4th, there is a new insistence on prayer:

> *Gladys, God listens with very much intensity, to His children in their prayer. Those who do not pray are numerous. They are enemies of the Lord. God will build on those who love Him, those whose every work is good for the Lord. Glory to the Lord!* (#1800).

On February 8, 1990, the Blessed Virgin gave Gladys a message which summarized everything: love, conversion, thanksgiving, and joy which resulted from it:

> *Pray during this novena so that there may never be any doubt about the love of the Father for His children. Pray so that every day there will be more converts. Pray, for the souls who do not pray, that they not move away from God. Praised be He! Read Isaiah 51:3:*
>
> *Yes, Yahweh consoles Zion. He consoles all its ruins. He makes its desert like an Eden; its steppe, like a garden of Yahweh. One finds there happiness and joy.* (#1802).

This joy, which underlies more than 1,800 messages of hope, signals the end to the messages in San Nicolás.

The last two messages are brief encouragements to hope, coupled with a blessing. The next to the last message, on February 10, 1990:

> *I tell my dear children: thank the Lord because of the faith which you have embraced. Let hope remain alive in your hearts. The Lord offers it to you; be conscious about it. It deals with a richness of which God makes you a present. Amen. Amen. Read Hebrews 10:23. Preach it, my daughter.* (#1803).

Last message, February 11, 1990, anniversary of the first apparition of Our Lady of Lourdes:

> *My dear children, I suggest that you follow my instructions step by step. Pray, make reparation, have faith! Blessed are those who look for refuge for their souls in prayer. Blessed are those who make reparation for the grave offenses which my Son receives. Blessed are those who have faith in the love of this mother. All those who have faith in God and in Mary will be saved. Glory to God. Preach it.* (#1804).

Since that time, the apparitions continue every day but without a "message." The interviews between Gladys and the Blessed Virgin have not ceased. They are not "secrets," but they only concern her and she does not render an account, except to her spiritual director.

## *Evolution*

If one looks for an evolution in the messages, one could discern three principal stages in them:

1. The choice and the preparation of the instrument, Gladys, for her mission; and already, the progressive and insistent request for the sanctuary. The Blessed Virgin actually points out its building site.

2. She creates a climate of hope and pursues a prophetic catechesis. She talks to mankind of today with their anguish and their sufferings in order to give them hope by placing it where it should be: in Christ Savior, in God. The Words of Jesus are associated with those of Mary about once a month, beginning November 15, 1983, in order to create a dynamism of conversion and of spiritual force.

   The construction of the sanctuary calls for a restoration of the Church, the Body of Christ. Its means are: constant prayer, rosary, penance, sacrifice, fasting, and the fundamental virtues of the Kingdom of God: faith, love, humility, docility, trust. Mary invites us to have recourse to the sacraments—privileged channels of the grace of God.

3. The third stage is the invitation by Mary to the consecration. She mentions it on February 2nd, the Feast of the Presentation. It is the consecration of Christ, and of the shrine itself.

## *Synthesis*

If one would dare to summarize this message of life and of victory, it would be that in a world headed toward perdition, Mary comes to the help of her children. For that, she chooses a people ready to welcome her: San Nicolás in Argentina. She comes under the sign of *Apocalypse* 12: *a woman clothed with the sun,* that is, with Christ, the Son of Justice in the struggle against the devil. She, in whom Christ came to dwell as the new Ark of the Covenant, comes to restore this covenant and prepare for the return of Christ.

She comes as a mother, and it is this title that she gives herself in order to express her concerns and family mediations. For she is, with the same heart, mother of Christ and mother of mankind, in a total solidarity. She is also the Church, place of the presence of Christ among us.

She renews her presence, misunderstood by mankind, by three signs: the statue—which had been abandoned in the dust of the belfry, a medal with her effigy, and the new sanctuary, place of the presence of Christ.

Through these signs and through her exhortations, she came to restore unity (covenant), through faith and hope, prayer (especially the Holy Rosary), conversion and penance, through the Word of the Eucharist, through fraternal love which is its fruit, and through consecration. This deification of grace is so forgotten in our secularized world, which has lost its sacred aura. For that she invites us to trust and hope, for God is stronger than all the threats or snares of the devil.

She invites us to put ourself under the domain of the Spirit. She speaks in the name of Christ, and in a constant dialogue with Him, in order to lead us to Him. In San Nicolás as previously, she actualizes her words to the servants of the wedding at Cana: *"Do whatever He tells you."* (*Jn.* 2:5).

Beyond the vicissitudes of this world, of which she gives a prophetic vision, she guides disoriented history completely toward the Trinity, to the Light of the Eternal Love which alone will subsist.

*CHAPTER 12*

# Authenticity

## *Traditional Criteria*

The apparitions of San Nicolás indeed verify the traditional criteria of the Church for the authenticity of apparitions (criteria stated precisely by Cardinal Seper, Prefect of the *Congregation of the Faith,* on February 25, 1979). It is very clear for Fr. Pérez and for Bishop Castagna in their demanding pastoral discernment. Following them, I recognize the same evidence:

— Faith and morals are illustrated faultlessly by the messages and the worship in San Nicolás.
— The signs speak to the crowds, notably the cures of which we have already spoken. They are in the process of examination. It would be premature to give exact information. Likewise for the exceptional signs which have exerted an influence on the movement of conviction and conversions: mysterious lights and perfumes.
— The sincerity and the psychological health of the visionary, examined by doctors of the Commission, do not present a problem and are gauges of credibility.

Let us especially consider the principal criterion which Christ Himself has taught us—*the fruits*—in the visionary, among the pilgrims, and beyond.

## *Gladys*

Gladys, the visionary, is first of all a sign by her discretion. And that invites us to respect her privacy, and not to speak about it. And yet, her authenticity is important to the credibility of San Nicolás, since she is the only witness of the message. May she forgive us. . .and may the readers leave her in peace.

When I spoke with her, I was able to verify what others have perceived, in a more consistent way: a balanced blossoming, a life of deep prayer, total communion with Christ. She thus found a true retreat with respect to the small things in life, be they adversities.

The mystical texts, which she wrote for herself, are not literature. They express a knowledge and an intimate experience with God—her way with Him. On reading these messages and some of the spiritual texts which she wrote, more and more frequently, I was attracted to one thing: the writing of this woman, who had so little schooling (until her eleventh year), is not unpolished and juvenile writing, but personal, free, harmonious. She expresses a radiant personality. With her, mysticism makes up for culture.

The expert graphologist of the Episcopal Commission confirmed her stability. Her writing shows the following qualities as determined by the Commission:

> "A notable intelligence, which could not be cultivated. A natural intelligence without intellectualism. Great lucidity (order and precision in ideas and concepts), which makes her master of her feelings and her instincts.
>
> "She acquires her information slowly and with difficulty, but once it has been acquired, she does not forget. She has an overall picture, without disparaging details.
>
> "She is careful in everything that she does. Her thought is always centered on the accom-

plishment of her tasks. She does not use her time economically, nor the effort that it would require of her.

"Less gifted for creativity and ideas, than for a logic which accomplishes.

"She possesses teaching skills: clarity, ability to explain correctly.

"With respect to affectivity, what characterizes her is ingenuity, sincerity, candor and loyalty. She is modest by religious and spiritual conviction. She has simple tastes. Her character is generous, prodigal, outgoing.

"She approaches others with very great facility. In it, she involves her qualities of sweetness and appeal. She is confident. Calmness and levelheadedness dominate in her. She is optimistic and joyful, and does not allow herself to be driven by impulses. She knows how to control them without losing her effective warmth.

"Outgoing with intimate friends, she is reserved and capable of keeping a secret. Her aspirations are high. Her lack of relief and personal initiative is bound to her sense of duty, and to her ability to sacrifice, which brings about an eclipse of her own ego.

"She is manually dexterous. She has a taste for the beautiful. Her personality is influenced by traditional, maternal tendencies, which include the past.

"With respect to her relationship to the world which surrounds her, her adaptation to new situations is easy. Her vital attitude is extroverted, and that is translated through a certain euphoria, a love of life, a vivaciousness of spirit, with hope and good humor. She takes the initiative in her relations and the influence of the environment is moderate.

> "The shock of obstacles and difficulties does not lead her to abandonment, but drives her to exceed herself. They hurt her pride and stimulate her. She can impose herself, or submit herself to others, according to what is convenient to her position and her situation.
>
> "She will obey her superiors and will be inflexible in her ethical and moral convictions.
>
> "Reasonable in discussion, she knows how to take up an opponent's point of view, recognize his errors, and give an objective value to the merit of the other. In her conduct, she is thrifty and leads a modest form of life. She knows how to consciously cut down expenditures, even more than her wishes.
>
> "Briefly, this personality appears gifted, with a profound goodness and limpidity of spirit and sense of justice. With clarity she knows how to place her talents in the service of God and of those around her.
>
> "She enjoys a mental, affective, and sexual health which the majority cannot attain" (abridged from the report of Mrs. Mata Torres, graphologist to the Commission of Inquiry of Msgr. Castagna).

I submitted a sample of this same writing, unfortunately without a signature, to a French graphologist at a higher level (an approved expert with the courts and tribunals). In spite of the limitations of the document, Mr. J. A. Muenier, who did not know anything about the identity and the personality of Gladys, confirmed and thoroughly studied the analysis of his Argentine colleague (whom he did not know).

— TEMPERAMENT: "Very internalized temperament with restrained impulses.

— SENSITIVITY: "Very vibrant sensitivity masked behind a very cold appearance. The writer is hardened against her sensitivity which is vulnerable by substituting some positive strengths, which have taken the place of negative elements.

— CHARACTER: "Of a spartan firmness, demanding, up to the point of being inexorable, capable of an exceptional courage in critical circumstances.

— "Possesses a strength of conviction which is as if indestructible, and which contrasts with a certain apparent fragility [. . .]

— PERSONALITY: "Receiving everything from interiorly, her perceptions or private revelations, rather secret, of which she does not like to give testimony. It does not matter how, for she is diametrically opposed to all 'hysteria,' to all exhibitionism. The human comedy, or the social 'controversy,' simulation, the investigation of the effect, do not interest her. She is incapable of being influenced by futilities, pettiness, formal conventionalities. She detests the grandiose. She is discreet, reticient, consistent, in spite of her extreme, highly serious sensitivity, and of very great dignity and sincerity.

— COMMUNICATION: "Very receptive behind an impassive appearance, but not to anything: to the real values of the spirit and the soul. She can go far in the perception of certain interior hidden revelations, reserved to a small minority of initiates. She has a great interior fervor. She speaks if it is really necessary, but she does not need to. Its substance is very rich. Her feelings are very intense, often secretly painful, very deep. She could be a great mystic, or become one.

"This writing reveals a grave, deep, respectful, sincere conscience filled with interior emotion, very discreet and modest, of being like the depository of a sacred message which one must take up and protect to the utmost, and especially not bring into repute. More secondarily and contradictorily, this same writing also reveals the need to be reassured, vis-a-vis, certain very secret, personal torments, about which she can only open up to her very rare confidants, exercising a religious function."

(The Muenier report, based on a "letter in Spanish" of a "writer of unknown age." He repeated this diagnosis, without knowing anything about Gladys except this document.)

As for the content, her spiritual, inspired writings are a constant living reference to God, to Christ. They reveal an undoubtable deep experience.

The fasting, which she pursues with ease, is a good sign of the authenticity of her prayer and her union with God.

The stigmata (medically verified: above, pages 22-25 of the manuscript), are a sign of the union with Christ, on His Cross itself, in the wake of Francis of Assisi. Her prayer is humble and in total communion with the intentions of God. She has no other desire than to serve Him.

## The Pilgrims

This grace of the messages spreads to the pilgrims who come to San Nicolás. The prayer there is calm, prolonged, intense, unceasing. Confessions are numerous. Every 25th of the month, they summon 20 to 25 confessors at the Campito. But it is not enough. They would need twice that number. The conversions are numerous and profound. A communicative joy reigns.

This grace is lasting. The pilgrims of San Nicolás have formed thousands of prayer groups throughout Argentina which exert their influence. This movement has inspired a number of vocations.

## Daughters of Mary

Msgr. Castagna, bishop of San Nicolás, authorized the first movement for a new order to be in charge of the sanctuary: the *Daughters of Mary of the Rosary of San Nicolás* (December 28, 1987). I was able to meet the first three sisters who so discreetly, so strongly, encouraged prayer at the sanctuary. The excessive prudence which exists in San Nicolás led me to delete their names in the interview which follows. Sister M., the one in charge, explained to me:

> "Our spirituality is basically contemplative but without enclosure. We pray the liturgy of the hours, meditate on the Word of God, do spiritual reading and adore the Blessed Sacrament. We attend Mass and say the three parts of the Rosary.
>
> "We want to live a life of interior and exterior poverty.
>
> "Our specific apostolate is catechesis and the Word of God. Since May 13th of last year, I have been encouraging a group of young people, from 14 to 17 years of age, for doctrinal formation, prayer, adoration, Rosary."
>
> "How do you recruit these young people?" I asked.
>
> "Mary leads them to us."

Sister B. explained the work of the sanctuary to me, particularly entrusted during the novena which precedes the twenty-fifth of each month:

> "We have a small room where we give informal talks to groups of 20 to 30, particularly the sick."

Sister Y. (the third sister) told me:

> "We founded the *Spiritual Associates of the Blessed Virgin* [Socios espirituales de la Virgen]: the sick who offer their sufferings. The first Wednesday of the month is specially consecrated to the sick and the handicapped of San Nicolás. We formed a group of lay people in order to help us with the liturgical calendar of events of the sanctuary. We give them theological and spiritual

> instruction. Each day, we encourage the recitation of the Rosary, especially during the novena, in harmony with the given message."

"We do not develop an intellectual, but a contemplative theology," stated Sister M., and she quoted these words from Gladys: "St. Francis said that he was ignorant, and that the Cross had taught him everything."

She observed: "For me it is exactly the same thing."

She took her theological studies at UNSTA (University of the North of St. Thomas Aquinas, operated by the Dominicans).

> "The Blessed Virgin teaches me the wisdom of the heart. Blessed is my ignorance which receives so much grace," she concluded.

The community is growing. At the beginning of April 1990, a postulant and three aspirants joined the first three sisters.

*CHAPTER 13*

# Conclusion And The Future

The apparitions in San Nicolás are the phenomenon of only one visionary. Neither she, nor Fr. Pérez, rector of the sanctuary, have taken into consideration the possibility of other "visionaries," even if the antennae of certain pilgrims perceive some small unverified signs, notably perfumes and lights.

The confrontation of the visionaries, so harassed in Medjugorje, does not have its place here. But the visionary, simple, discreet, balanced, serious, solid, is up to the task. She is living a spiritual development of high quality.

## *An Education*

The bishop has received this popular movement, which is also a movement of grace, in an exemplary way. His pastoral prudence inspired a discernment in him, where the critical sense is constantly at the service of a mature spiritual meaning.

He dedicated himself to stimulate good fruits, which have multiplied. His critical sense chose experts from a most varied background, including minds who were prejudiced, or closed to the apparitions. He recorded their differences and contradictory points of view, and respected their freedom in the service of an open judgment, which slowly matured.

For a long time, people had thought that the most normal attitude with respect to visionaries was to contradict them, and to put them on trial, for "contradiction obtains the best proof that God is there."

Such a principle is dangerous. At times it has demolished or caused deviation in those who were its victims. Even an authentic visionary does not necessarily have a charisma of stability and solidity. They can be fragile. The Church should help them in this difficult task, and not lead them into temptation. It is to tempt God then, to place them in an impossible situation, for we defy the Creator in order to produce His trials. God does not perform His miracles on request. He acts in life. Life is important then. One must cultivate it, above all.

The problem is the same as in education. In the past, it was strictly rigid and harsh. It tested the most solid ones, but discouraged or hurt the others, and left them with complexes of inferiority or instability. To educate is to awaken, channel, instruct, but also to protect, maintain, stimulate to the utmost, the resources of those whom one tries to teach.

Such is the attitude that has prevailed in San Nicolás. The constructive pastoral has helped the visionary, and the people of God, to better find their spiritual development and health through an array of converging means.

The apparitions and devotion to Our Lady have gradually rallied the minds. The municipality of San Nicolás made a gift of the Campito. The population supports the apparitions. The 150,000 inhabitants constitute the majority of the monthly pilgrimage. This influence won over the archbishop, who had originally come simply as a witness and pilgrim, after the Episcopal Conference first addressed the event.

This type of unanimity is part of the grace of San Nicolás. The climate has been so much more favorable, that many bishops have verified the fruits of San Nicolás in the prayer groups of their dioceses.

## *Will the Apparitions Be Recognized?*

Then, one will ask, when is the bishop going to recognize the apparitions?

This is without great importance. For the official recognition of an apparition does not make it a dogma, necessary for salvation. No one is obliged to believe in a recognized apparition, even Lourdes and Fatima which received the best guarantees. An apparition does not have as its function, the promotion of a new dogma, but to awaken the faith, charity, and especially hope. Thomas Aquinas stressed these points, and that the function of apparitions is essentially prophetic.

These apparitions are an interpolation of Our Lady directed to the hearts of mankind with complete freedom. The effective recognition of authenticity has less importance than the fruits.

Msgr. Castagna took over San Nicolás from within, in the service of the Lord. He guides and confirms this movement of grace. He confirms the direction of the faithful, who were the first to discern these apparitions, with generosity and thanksgiving.

An apparition is above all, a pastoral problem, and its approval comes in addition; it confirms the (sensus fidelium) which was first awakened.

If the people of San Nicolás and Argentina continue this large and prayerful adherence, recognition of the apparition will not be necessary, or, it will be plucked like a ripe and ready fruit.

According to the criteria established by Rome, bishops are invited to recognize (or not), apparitions at two stages:

1. Recognition of the *worship,* which popular fervor creates at the place of the apparition;
2. Recognition of the apparition itself and of its authenticity.

1. At the first stage, the bishop of San Nicolás did not publish any official approval of the worship, but he gradually participated in the worship: processions, sermons, Masses. He built and inaugurated the sanctuary. He had the statue transferred there. He invited the archbishop there, who became an examplary pilgrim of Our Lady. It was the best and the most fruitful way to endorse the events in the very life of the community. For it is life that counts—that of the Body of Christ, which is the Church. In this way, the tree of San Nicolás bears fruit in abundance. In San Nicolás, the worship is recognized **de facto**, because the bishop has taken it up and provided leadership in prayer. It does not appear that a juridical recognition would add importance to it (said without denying its eventual opportunity).

2. For conscience's sake, I asked the bishop whether it was important to officially recognize the apparitions themselves. This question is not among his current concerns. It is premature. He had named a commission, which continues serious and multi-disciplinary inquiries, by calling largely on experts (theologians, biblical scholars, psychologists, graphologists, doctors), favorable or unfavorable to the apparitions. It can normally lead to an official recognition of authenticity, but that is another stage (secondary and even accessory to grace and to life). It will impose itself better then if the event is allowed to mature calmly and fruitfully in the people of God. Then this statement will come—less in giving authorization and cutting polemics than as a thanksgiving and a feast; the official recognition and thanksgiving.

That will perhaps be the logical outcome of the event some day; but it is not up to us to anticipate the decisions of Msgr. Castagna, vicar of Christ by divine right in San Nicolás. But to interpret the facts, and his thoughts, by saying that the event presents itself well, in spite of objections of some experts, largely constitutes the present state of affairs.

## Local or Universal Implications

A final question may be asked. It worried me on the plane during the flight to Buenos Aires, and accompanied my whole inquiry:

> "There are so many apparitions today. I do not think that all of them can have the permanent and universal merit of Lourdes and Fatima. This multiplicity itself invites one to think that the majority of apparitions and supernatural phenomena have a local implication: the decentralization of apparitions spares Christians long trips, since Our Lady knocks at their door."

What is there about it in San Nicolás? Does the sanctuary have a diocesan calling? National? Latin American? World?

Our Lady's plan is to reside in the sanctuary and to convert a city, a people, and beyond. But on several occasions she referred to the whole world. What should we think about it?

For now, the audience is principally national. Argentina accepts the event: from the north, to the polar region of the south, and from the Atlantic to the Cordillera of the Andes, thousands of prayer groups have been founded, and all of that has already stimulated a renewal of vocations, notably in San Nicolás, where a seminary is under construction to house 30 seminarians.

On August 5, 1985, Gladys saw in the heavens the blue and white flag of her country, accompanied by a larger flag which was completely blue—the color of the mantle of the Blessed Virgin. The latter commented:

> *The fact is that I protect your country. I protect Argentina. This message concerns your people.* (#633).

Beyond this national calling, does the sanctuary have an international and world calling? Two particulars seem to address this issue:

1. Some pilgrims are already coming from neighboring countries, and at times, from farther away.
2. The messages themselves seem to be addressed not only to Argentina, but to the world.

It would be premature to pass judgment on this point. It is the reception (as theologians say), that is to say, the spontaneous welcome of Christians, which will decide this implication. The (sensus fidelium) is the judge on these matters. That is why it is good to spread the initial information, which gives opportunities for a wide dissemination and allows each one the opportunity to discern.

The apparitions are only episodes and particular facts in the life of the Church. They are not at all the essential, as are the Gospel and the Sacraments, dogmas and charity. They are a contribution, a stimulant to the faith and especially to hope, as we have seen. Particular attractions and devotions are left to the discernment of each one in the Church, which is a place of freedom. Christians adhere to them according to their affinities, and especially according to the inspiration of the Holy Spirit.

If the message speaks to French-speaking countries (not very open to apparitions and dissuaded on all sides) and if the messages bear the same fruits as in Argentina, then it will be useful to edit the whole of the messages with the understanding that they are a viaticum—a stage in our route, but not a founding and permanent monument, like the Bible. Still, these messages are recommended for their balanced doctrine, their taste, their spiritual quality, and the fruits borne in Argentina.

The future will tell:

— To what extent the apparitions are a temporary or lasting grace (as the construction of a large sanctuary requested by Our Lady already attests), and if local grace for Argentina, or for the universal Church?

— What the extent and importance of this grace will be.

The gifts of God confuse the expectations and the wisdom of men. Through the sense of the faithful, and the judgment of the bishop, discernment comes about. Still, it is God Who will decide.

# Supplement #1

**Report of the Commission of Inquiry named by Msgr. Castagna concerning the events related to the statue of "Our Lady of the Rosary of San Nicolás," which is found in the cathedral.**

*October 25, 1985*

## *Brief Historical Synthesis*

Since its beginning, the parish of the city of San Nicolás de Los Arroyos, province of Buenos Aires, Republic of Argentina, has been the center of a deep piety towards the Most Blessed Virgin honored under the title of "Our Lady of the Rosary." She has been the first patroness of the curé de Los Arroyos.

The existing cathedral of San Nicolás de Bari was inaugurated in 1884. On this occasion, someone had offered a beautiful statue of Our Lady of the Rosary, from Rome, which Pope Leo XIII had especially blessed for the parishioners of San Nicolás. At that time, the *Confraternity of the Rosary* had been founded, and every year they celebrated the Feast of the Most Blessed Virgin as well as a preparatory novena.

Now, recently, on September 25, 1983, in this city of San Nicolás, there began an event of exceptional character. A simple lady, Gladys Quiroga de Motta, 48 years of age, married, and mother of two daughters, who was not able to finish her elementary studies, and who had no theological or biblical knowledge, is said to have seen and heard the Most Blessed Virgin Mary. The description of the apparition coincided with that of the statue of "Our Lady of the Rosary," which was venerated in the parish church.

According to this person, the Most Blessed Virgin continuously asked for the construction of a church in her honor at a determined place. This person also stated that the Most Blessed Virgin began to give her a whole series of messages, especially of exhortation with biblical references, and calls to prayer and to conversion.

## Naming of the Commission

Since an inquiry was indispensable, as well as further expertise and consultation, the bishop named a commission which consisted of priests from his diocese. This commission worked according to a pre-established plan as follows:

1. Study of the psycho-physical health of Mrs. Motta.
2. Study of the writings of Mrs. Motta, called "messages."
3. Exhaustive investigation of the cures which had an apparent relation to these events.

Since it was presided by its bishop, this commission convened frequently. This is what was accomplished according to the pre-established plan.

A. For the inquiry on psycho-physical health of Mrs. Motta, they consulted a psychologist, two graphologists, and an entire team of psychiatrists and psychologists from the Faculty of Psychology of Salvador (Jesuits). They separately conducted an exhaustive work and made their conclusions known:

The graphologists worked directly on the writings of Mrs. Motta—her notes after locutions and apparitions.

The psychiatrists and psychologists came from Buenos Aires to San Nicolás on several occasions to examine Mrs. Motta.

B. At the request of the Commission the presumed messages were always examined by an exegete and a theologian, as well as by other experts competent on the subject. All presented their report in a clear and detailed fashion.

C. With respect to the presumed cures, as the news of them presented itself, the Commission required, for each case, the clinical history, medical information, the therapy in progress, and the results which had been obtained.

## *The Current Situation*

Mrs. Motta has always been and remains in contact with the bishop [. . .]. She maintains her distance with those people who wish to meet her. In other respects, she writes down the daily messages, which are received regularly since the beginning of October 1983, until today.

Results of the psycho-physical investigations: nothing permits one to suppose the presence of a psycho-pathological alienation, or of a hallucinatory process. Not delirious or illusory, capable of establishing the loss of contact with reality. The personality of Mrs. Motta strikes us by its good balance, in perfect harmony with reality.

After consultation and evaluation, the writings do not present any theological objection. One of the reports commented on their harmony with Holy Scripture and their pedagogical resources.

With respect to the cures which have been presumed until today, the dossier of a particular case, whose clinical history was requested at the time, arrived, but still incomplete. The case in question included serious testimonies.

Furthermore, through the ordinance of August 25, 1985, the municipality of the city of San Nicolás granted to the bishopric, land destined for the construction of the sanctuary in honor of "Our Lady of the Rosary." Mrs. Motta wrote that this land was destined for this objective.

## *Pastoral Program*

The bishop, as well as the Commission, approved the need to program the pastoral of the event. For that purpose, the bishop chose the curé of the parish, where the parcel of land ceded by the municipality was, so that he might organize and orient the religious ceremonies and the recitation of the Most Holy Rosary.

On the feast days dedicated to the Most Blessed Virgin, and particularly the 25th of each month when atendance by the pilgrims increased in the Cathedral, the schedules of Masses and confessions were spread out during the day. During the preachings related to the Blessed Virgin, it was decided that every allusion, direct to the apparitions themselves, would be avoided.

At the present time, it is permitted to print images and the messages. The necessary steps were taken in order to obtain the editorial ownership.

Only the Blessed Virgin is important (in this matter). Thus it is only about her—her devotion and veneration.

Upon the request of the diocesan bishop, *the Commission of study and of discernment on the subject of the events relative to the statue of Our Lady of the Rosary of San Nicolás,* which was found in the Cathedral of San Nicolás, presented this report on October 25, 1985.

# Supplement #2

**Letter from Mariqui to her cousin Maria Teresa de Maiztegui on the cure of her son Gonzalo.**

*Pergamino, June 2, 1985*

Dear Teresita,

How happy I am to write to you! You have seen the article which appeared in *La Nacion* [of Buenos Aires], which narrated the cure of Gonzalo but under another name. Raoul [my husband], did not want to make his name public or the city in which we live, in order to reserve all importance to the same event: that is to say, the hand of Our Lady of the Rosary, which performed this cure.

This is what happened to Gonzalo. The first symptoms [of the illness] appeared on [Friday] October 19, 1984, and we consulted here, in Pergamino, without any results. On [Thursday] October 25, 1984, we were in Rosario. The first tomography was done there. The diagnosis was the following: a tumor with a left frontal cystic lesion having a mass effect, undoubtedly congenital, caused pressure on this whole area, concluding a paralysis of the right side. Gonzalo was in a permanent state of somnolence. He did not speak and hardly moved. The treating doctor confirmed this diagnosis: cerebral tumor the size of an egg. For Gonzalo, the only chance for survival was an operation with some irreversible neurological after effects.

It was undoubtedly after that, while walking in the corridors of the Spanish hospital, I was weighed down for a second between the baby which I was carrying in me and the gravity of the present instant which was Gonzalo. It was then that I entrusted myself into the hands of the Most Blessed Virgin. I only asked her for the strength necessary to face what was going to happen—life or death, and thus to be able to transmit it to those who were dear to me. From that moment on, a great peace invaded me and it permitted me to concern myself with my child with all the serene strength of a mother.

*Monday, October 29, 1984*—cerebral arteriography. The paralysis of the right side attained its maximum level. Gonzalo did not make a move in his bed. His right side was cold, frozen, deprived of life. It was undoubtedly the most painful night! Previously, we had requested the Last Sacraments for Gonzalo, as well as the Eucharist, although he had not yet finished his preparation for First Communion, since he was only seven.

*Tuesday, October 30, 1984*—10:30. The priest arrived. It was Fr. Busso. He spoke to him, and explained to him that he was going to receive Jesus, and Gonzalo prepared himself with a great interior strength. He was placed under the protection of the Most Blessed Virgin of the Rosary of San Nicolás. It was from this moment that the change began (or the miracle). Forty-five minutes later the paralysis began to give way. The state of torpor was less evident. Coloring appeared on his face.

*Thursday, November 1, 1984*—exactly 7 days later, second tomography. Result: the zone of hypodensity recorded at the beginning was clearly smaller (70 percent) and the mass effect disappeared.

The causes? . . . We do not know them and they cannot be explained. For the first time the doctor speaks of not operating. He reduces the doses of medication.

*Friday, November 2, 1984*—lumbar puncture with all the tests which accompanied it. The encephalo-rachidian liquid was clear as water (in my opinion!). I asked Gonzalo, since he carried the Child Jesus in his heart, to offer Him this suffering so as to be able to be cured very soon. No complaint came from my son's mouth. The result of the analysis was excellent.

*Saturday, November 3, 1984*—the amount of medication was reduced. He walked, he played at times. He sees, and he remains awake longer. During the following days, improvement continued. He read.

*Wednesday, November 7, 1984*—They reduced the amount of cortisone to one tablet a day. Gonzalo was walking. He used the right hand very little, stressing his use of the left hand.

*Thursday, November 8, 1984*—no more medication.

*Friday, November 9, 1984*—He walks by himself. In the meantime, his right side has less strength: arms, hand, and right leg. We could leave the hospital and return home.

*Monday, November 19, 1984*—third tomography: in place of pervasive hypodense mass, there was only a scar.

Conclusion: at the present time, his recuperation is rapid and progressive for the limp of his right side. He writes with his right hand. There is no lesion on his intellectual side. He understands perfectly. No more trace of inhibitions (he was previously timid, austere, introverted).

After that, Teresita, I marvel each day in the presence of the miracle of his life, which has been recovered. I thank the Most Blessed Virgin of the Rosary who made use of Gonzalo to show her mercy immeasurably. Attached is a copy of the messages of the Blessed Virgin. With all my heart I say to you: each time that I will go to San Nicolás, I will place your intentions at the feet of the Blessed Virgin. I am so happy that after so many years, we have found each other again. I will be waiting for you whenever you wish.

All my affection for Coco and the children. I hug you most affectionately.

Mariqui

(It is the familiar name of Maria del Valle Godoy de Miguel.)

(Gonzalo is 13 years old at the time I am writing this book. Right now, he is taller than his father. He is in perfect physical, psychic, and intellectual health.)

# Supplement #3

## *Chronology of San Nicolás*

**1983**

| | |
|---|---|
| September 25 | First apparition of the Blessed Virgin to Gladys Quiroga de Motta. |
| September 28 | Second apparition |
| October 7 | Gladys asks the Blessed Virgin what she desires. She receives the vision of a chapel. |
| October 12 | Gladys confides in a priest. |
| October 13 | The Blessed Virgin speaks to her for the first time. |
| October | Audience with the diocesan bishop: Msgr. Antonio F. Rossi. |
| November 15 | Gladys receives the message: *I am the patroness of this region. Assert my rights.* |
| November 15 | First locution from Christ. Since then, He appeared once a month with a message, which prolonged or commented on that of the Blessed Virgin. |
| November 19 | The Blessed Virgin makes her mission known to Gladys: *You are a bridge of unity; Preach my words.* |
| November 24 | A ray of light shows Gladys the building site of the future temple. |
| November 27 | She sees the statue of "Our Lady of the Rosary," consigned to the bottom of the cathe- |

dral belfry after a hand had been broken. She recognizes the effigy of the apparition. The Blessed Virgin tells her: *I want to settle on the bank of the Paraná.*

**1984**

| | |
|---|---|
| August 28 | Msgr. Castagna, born in 1931, ordained to the episcopacy in 1978, auxiliary bishop of Buenos Aires, was named bishop of San Nicolás. |
| October 30 | 10:30, first Communion of little Gonzalo on his death bed, and the beginning of his cure. |
| November | First audience with the Pope concerning the events at San Nicolás. |

**1985**

| | |
|---|---|
| April | Nomination of the Episcopal Commission of Inquiry. |
| April 25 | The municipality presents the Campito as a gift to the bishopric. |
| October 25 | Statement of the Investigation Commission (above, supplement 1). |

**1986**

| | |
|---|---|
| February 25 | First monthly procession on the anniversary of the first apparition. This procession, followed by a celebration of Mass on the Campito, will take place in the future each month on the same date. |
| March 25 | Second procession and Mass, presided by the bishop of the place, Msgr. Castagna. |
| May | Disclosure of the medal. |
| August 25 | Msgr. Castagna presides again over the procession and the monthly Mass. He announces the laying of the cornerstone of the sanctuary. |
| September 10 | Adoption of the plan. |
| September 23 | Formation of the Pro Templo Commission. |
| September 25 | Laying of the cornerstone of the sanctuary. |

| | |
|---|---|
| September | The first publication of the magazine on the sanctuary: *Maria del Rosario de San Nicolás. Revista del Santuario, no. 1.* |
| October 25 | Inauguration of the house of pilgrims and of a dissemination center. |

**1987**

| | |
|---|---|
| April 11 | At Rosario, Msgr. Castagna has an audience with the Pope (who was visiting Argentina). The Pope asks the pilot of the helicopter to descend over the sight for the sanctuary. |
| August | Beginning of the printing works of the Center. |
| October 8 | Signing of the contract with the construction company of Gerlach and Campbell. |
| October 13 | The starting of the construction of the sanctuary. |

**1988**

| | |
|---|---|
| October 5 | End of the first stage of the construction of the sanctuary. |

**1989**

| | |
|---|---|
| March 19 | Inauguration and blessing of the first part of the sanctuary (the nave, built only as far as the transept). The statue of Our Lady was transferred there. Fr. Carlos Pérez, curé of the cathedral, was named rector of the new sanctuary. |
| Beginning of August | My first trip to San Nicolás. |
| September 25 | Msgr. Castagna ordains a priest, Carlitos, a deacon who has been assigned to the sanctuary along with Fr. Pérez and Fr. Pablo, OSB. |

**1990**

| | |
|---|---|
| February 2 | The work begins again (second section) in spite of the inflation which stymies the donations and forces them to depend on hope. |

| | |
|---|---|
| February 11 | Last public mesage of Our Lady in San Nicolás. |
| April 2 | Pilgrimage to San Nicolás by Dom Gobbi, founder of the *Marian Movement of Priests.* Nearly 60,000 priests gather. |
| August 3-6 | My second trip to San Nicolás. |
| October | Msgr. Castagna elected by the Argentine bishops to represent the Episcopal Conference at the Synod in Rome. |

# Supplement #4

## *Medical Bureau and Healings*

Doctors Eduardo Juan Telechea, Martinez Derita, and Pelliciota have established a medical bureau which has solicited the aid of several specialists.

Dr. Telechea told me during my trip in August, 1990, that among the numerous healings which have been established at the sanctuary, 10 cases, which have been better documented, lend themselves to a certified report, and are under study.

Here are some examples:

— Graciela CANET de Buron, 33 years old, had contracted at 6 years of age, a photo traumatism of both eyes while looking at an eclipse of the sun. Her vision was seriously damaged. In 1978, a retinography (back of the eye) had identified a lesion of the retina. In 1986 Dr. Nano, an ophthalmologist of the first class in Buenos Aires, declared it incurable. She made a pilgrimage to San Nicolás and prayed for her cure, and received, as an answer, the smell of perfume at the fifth station of the Stations of the Cross.

On her return to Buenos Aires, while walking on the street, she felt something and passed her hand over her eyes. She clearly saw with one eye. Several days later, the same healing of the other eye took place. She saw Dr. Nano again and he confirms the cure.

"The best thing in all of this is that since then we have begun to follow the Blessed Virgin. We have made the consecration, tried to accomplish everything that she asks for. We have received innumerable graces and have found true joy," she said in the testimony signed by her, her husband, and her two children.

— Oscar Arnaldo PAOLINI suffered (in February 1990), from a "difficulty in swallowing and from an aphasia" (impossibility of speaking). A biopsy of March 13, 1990, confirmed a cancer of the larynx (carcinoma). The operation, which had been set for March 26th at Pirovano Hospital in Buenos Aires, was postponed due to the general condition of the patient.

On April 15, they began a long treatment of chemotherapy. The sick person's niece, who had established a commercial travel organization in San Nicolás, remained on the bus while her clients prayed in the sanctuary. She suddenly remembered her sick uncle, came down from the bus, and went before the statue in order to pray for his cure. Since then (hardly had the first session of chemotherapy been conducted), the sick man felt cured. On May 15, 1990, medical examinations did not reveal any anomaly. He gained 10 kilos. His niece was converted.

— Rodrigo RINCIN (17 years old) suffered from a "bilateral urethral reflux," with an enormous bladder (the urine would go back toward the kidneys). They had to make an incision in the bladder (in order to eliminate this urine but the urethra was malfunctioning and the evacuation was insufficient.

In 1986, they tried the nephrotomy of the right kidney and twenty days later of the left kidney. This resulted in two fistulas of evacuation in the back. In April 1988, a new operation was set in order to implant a new urethra, but the doctor gave up the idea of doing it seeing the condition of the patient.

On July 25, 1989, Rodrigo's mother, on a pilgrimage to San Nicolás, confided her son's illness to Mary. He became cured. An x-ray examination of February 8, 1990, confirmed that the urethra had begun to function again. On March 6, 1990, the doctor removed the two fistulas which had been placed for the artificial discharge.

All these cases (and others) are under study, and the sick who have been cured give thanks to Mary.

# Supplement #5

**How to get to San Nicolás?**

## *Important Date*

Each 25th of the month, anniversary day of the first apparition, a procession in honor of the Blessed Virgin fills the streets of the district, during the hour which precedes the main Mass. The Mass is usually celebrated by the bishop of San Nicolás. All of the cars which are parked around the Campito leave after the Mass.

The monthly celebration is preceded by a novena.

One does not dare encourage elderly people to attend on the 25th of September, anniversary of the first apparition, a day of great crowds. If one needs to move, it is necessary to accept the drudgery of endless lines. The same problem exists on May 25th, a national holiday: (the Revolution of May 1810 and the anniversary of May 25, 1810).

## *Means of Transportation*

AUTO: use the Buenos Aires-Rosario highway, by way of San Nicolás, a 3 hour drive. One can rent a car in Buenos Aires: (AVIS, Maipu 942, telephone 311-3899 or 8882).

TRAIN: the line from Buenos Aires to Rosario leaves from the Mitre Station: 3 trains a day, very old, except for the pullman cars.

BUSES: every day, every hour. Leave the Empresa Chevalier

in Buenos Aires, telephone 313-3264 and 313-3295. The Omnibus Terminal in Retiro: the large square of railway and bus stations in Buenos Aires.

## Pilgrimages

The *Mision Laica Argentina* (1130 Santa Fe Street, Sixth Floor, Office no. 21) organizes 5 pilgrimages a month, with morning departure and return the same evening. Telephone: 814-4205, 4206, 4207.

The pilgrimage of the *Esclavas de Maria* (1372 Montevideo Street, Buenos Aires 1018, telephone: 812-1735 and 42-1417) is particularly well organized. They recite the Rosary all along the way, going and coming. A guide prepares and explains the meaning of the process. He answers questions of the pilgrims and allows them to use the microphone to relate testimonies on the return trip. It is necessary to make reservations in advance, since the number of buses is determined according to the number of pilgrims. Four to ten buses usually leave each 25th of the month at 8 o'clock in the morning, and return after 4 o'clock in the afternoon in winter, 6 or 7 o'clock in the evening in summer, after Mass at the Campito. The hour varies according to the season.

## Lodging

(For information only) Hotel El Acuerdo, #7 Francia Street, telephone 04 612 7564. One will find economic and adequate food at the Club Social, on Mire Square (Square of the Cathedral), in the garden.

## Books and Medals

At the Centro Mariano (Marian Center), near the sanctuary, one can obtain books, pictures and medals.

You can find a place for a picnic, and some restrooms, at approximately 200 meters from the sanctuary (415 Francia Street).

# How to Help in the Construction of the Sanctuary?

San Nicolás is above all, a spiritual message of conversion, prayer and hope. But (one cannot forget it), the Blessed Virgin has asked immediately for the swift construction of her sanctuary. Sky rising inflation, which came from the economic crisis, slows down this expensive project. Whoever wants to participate in this construction can send donations to the following addresses:

**In Argentina:**

*Comision Pro Templo,* Cassilla de Correo 79, 2900 San Nicolás, Argentina (by crossed check which can be deposited in any bank in Argentina).

The Comision Pro Templo has an account in different banks:

1. Banco de los Arroyos or Caja de Ahorros, account no. 9745/5 (branch in San Nicolás)
2. Banco de Galicia, account no. 177/5-177/9 (branch in San Nicolás)
3. Banco de la Nacion Argentina, account no. 11344/8 (branch in San Nicolás)
4. Banco de la Provincia de Buenos Aires, account Caja de Ahorros, no. 15605/1 (branch in San Nicolás)

**In the United States:**

Contributions for the construction of the Sanctuary may be made to The Riehle Foundation. Donations should be specifically marked:

"SANCTUARY CONSTRUCTION FUND"

and sent to:

THE RIEHLE FOUNDATION
P.O. BOX 7
MILFORD, OHIO 45150

Donations made to this account will be forwarded by bank transfer to the principal bank account in Argentina.

Faith Publishing Company has been organized as a service for the publishing and distribution of materials that reflect Christian values, and in particular the teachings of the Catholic Church.

It is dedicated to publication of only those materials that reflect such values.

Faith Publishing Company also publishes books for The Riehle Foundation. The Foundation is a non-profit, tax-exempt producer and distributor of Catholic books and materials worldwide, and also supplies hospital and prison ministries, churches and mission organizations.

For more information on the publications of Faith Publishing Company, or for additional copies of this book, AN APPEAL FROM MARY IN ARGENTINA, or the forthcoming book, THE MESSAGES OF OUR LADY AT SAN NICOLÁS, contact: